SHANGHAI PASSAGE

————————

SHANGHAI PASSAGE

* ———————————————— *

by Gregory Patent

Illustrations by Ted Lewin

Clarion Books

New York

Clarion Books
a Houghton Mifflin Company imprint
215 Park Avenue South, New York, NY 10003
Text copyright © 1990 by Gregory Patent
Illustrations copyright © 1990 by Ted Lewin

For information about permission to reproduce
selections from this book, write to Permissions,
Houghton Mifflin Company, 2 Park Street, Boston, MA 02108.
Printed in the USA

Library of Congress Cataloging-in-Publication Data
Patent, Greg, 1939-
Shanghai passage / by Gregory Patent
p.   cm.
Summary: The author's account of his childhood in Shanghai during
World War II and its aftermath.
ISBN 0-89919-743-4
1. Patent, Greg, 1939- —Juvenile literature.   2. Jews—China—
Shanghai—Biography—Juvenile literature.   3. World War, 1939-1945—
China—Shanghai—Personal narratives, Jewish—Juvenile literature.
4. Shanghai (China)—Biography—Juvenile literature.   [1. Patent,
Greg, 1939- . 2. Jews—China—Biography.   3. World War,
1939-1945—China—Shanghai—Personal narratives.]   I. Title.
DS135.C5P33   1990
951'.13200492402—dc20
[B]   89-31545
CIP
AC

HAL 10 9 8 7 6 5 4 3 2 1

For my parents, Mabel and Joe,
who somehow got us through it all.
For my two sons, David and Jason,
whose father could not be prouder of them.

———— * ————

And in loving memory of Ann Troy,
who first suggested the idea for this book.
Her gentle and sensitive editorial guidance
helped bring SHANGHAI PASSAGE
safely into port.

Contents

──────────────────────────

Preface

————————————————

ON MAY 5, 1939, I was born in the British Crown Colony of Hong Kong off the southeast coast of China. In 1934 my parents had met and fallen in love in Shanghai, China's largest city. They married and settled down there in 1935. Their backgrounds were very different. My mother was born in a suburb of Baghdad, Iraq, but had grown up in Hong Kong. My father was Russian. He had been raised in Irkutsk, Siberia. Although they came from completely different cultures, both were Jewish, so ultimately there was no objection to the marriage by either family.

Large numbers of foreigners resided in the great, bustling seaport city of Shanghai in the 1930s. It was the country's center for foreign trade and one of the most cosmopolitan cities in the world at that time. The foreigners with the highest status and power were the British. The French and Americans living there also had position, but some other nationalities, including the Iraqis and Russians, were not in the same league socially and economically.

My parents decided to have me born British so that I'd have all the advantages of a British citizen living in Shanghai, especially when I became an adult. That's why, when my mother was nine months pregnant, she boarded a ship to Hong Kong, accompanied by her mother and a cousin. Because Hong Kong belonged to England, my being born there automatically made me British. No one could have known then what an ironic plan this would turn out to be once World War II reached China.

A few days after my mother arrived, she gave birth to me in Matilda Hospital. When I was eight weeks old, my mother brought me, a British subject, to Shanghai. My future status in the city would be assured, my parents thought.

Shanghai was my home for almost eleven years—all through World War II, when the Japanese occupied the city; for a few years of peace afterward; at the Communist takeover of Shanghai; and during the first year of the Communist regime.

This is the story of my growing up there during those exciting, unpredictable years before my ultimate passage out of Shanghai—and out of my childhood.

SHANGHAI
PASSAGE
————————

CHAPTER ONE

Granny's Room

————————————

THE SUDDEN, LOUD WAIL of the air-raid siren startled us. My mother pulled me into the nearest doorway for safety, away from all the plate-glass windows facing the street. American planes had begun another air raid on Shanghai. Only this time we were caught right in the middle of it while strolling on Bubbling Well Road.

Almost immediately, Japanese antiaircraft guns began booming at the planes overhead. I covered my ears, trying to keep out the deafening sound. Right across the street, a poor Chinese worker dropped the rickshaw carriage he had been pulling and fell to the ground screaming. He had been hit by shrapnel, fragments of exploding shells from the antiaircraft guns. I watched in horror as streams of blood ran down his arms and legs. Frightened people were yelling and running in all directions. My mother turned my face away from the awful sight, and we huddled together until the antiaircraft guns stopped and the all-clear signal sounded.

Hurrying back to our home on Seymour Road seemed to take forever, even though we'd only walked about a block before the alarm sounded. We crossed the street, dodging a few bicyclists, and turned left at the Uptown Theatre on the corner. The entrance to the Cosmopolitan Apartments, where we lived, was just a few yards ahead. My mother and I ran hand in hand down the long lane leading to our building and up the two flights of stairs to our apartment.

The air-raid siren had scared Granny, too, and she gave me a big welcoming hug of relief when I rushed into the room. My mother told Granny in Arabic what had happened, while I sat on the couch and caught my breath. Both my parents had a tremendous fear of air raids because of what happened in Shanghai in 1937. Japan had been at war with China for several years. Japanese bombers destroyed large sections of the city, and one bomb that fell downtown killed about a thousand people. It took a long time for the area to be cleared up and for the rotting, charred bodies to be removed. My parents had to pass by the disaster as they walked to work each day.

Air raids were not uncommon in Shanghai during the summer of 1944. The Americans were getting closer to defeating Japan and ending World War II. Today's air raid had spoiled the trip my mother and

I were making to the YMCA library in downtown Shanghai. We often walked the two-mile distance to get books to read. I was five years old then, and the air raids always frightened me. What scared me most were the long siren blasts and the loud booms of the antiaircraft guns. Despite my fear, there was one thing I liked about the gunfire, and that was the black puffs of smoke it left suspended in the sky. I enjoyed seeing them gradually transform into streaks and then disappear. My parents, however, longed for the war to be over and for the Japanese to leave Shanghai.

———— * ————

The Cosmopolitan Apartments is the first home in Shanghai that I remember. It was actually Granny's apartment, but the war brought with it a housing shortage. So in late 1941 my mother, my father, and I moved in with her. Although English was not the native language of my parents or Granny, it was the only one my parents shared, so I grew up speaking it. What we spoke was really a variation of British English, with words like *lorry* for "truck," *lift* for "elevator," and *tiffin* for "lunch."

I called my mother and father Mummy and Daddy, the way English children addressed their parents. Everyone I knew called me Gigi—with the Gs pronounced as in *giggle,* because I giggled so much. Granny spoke Arabic with my mother, but the little English Granny understood made it possible for my father and me to converse with her.

I only knew my mother's mother as Granny and always called her that. She was a dear, kindhearted woman, and she cared for me as if I were her own child. Granny was in her fifties then, and she had gray hair that was always in a hairnet. In Iraq she had been married to a rabbi at the age of thirteen. The first of her children was born the following year, and she had four more by the time she was thirty. My mother was her youngest. At thirty-two Granny had become a widow.

Soon after, Granny and her children all moved to Hong Kong to live with Granny's brother-in-law. About ten years later, she and my mother came to Shanghai to live with some other relatives. By then, Granny's other children were married and already living in Shanghai.

Granny's apartment had just one room, about fifteen feet long and twelve feet wide, and it had to serve all our needs for over six years. It was kitchen, living room, bedrooms, dining room, and playroom all rolled into one. In one corner, a door led to a tiny bathroom. All cooking was done on a small gas stove near the front door.

An icebox—a white cabinet about four feet high on legs, with a door, some shelves, and an ice bin—completed the kitchen. Each day a coolie, or unskilled Chinese laborer, hauled a large slab of ice up the stairs and put it in the icebox for us. By then, the previous day's slab had melted, and the water was thrown away. We kept dairy products there to prevent them from spoiling. Usually we could only afford to buy what food we needed for the day, so leftovers weren't a concern. Mostly, the icebox was used to store water. Tap water was not safe to drink in Shanghai, so Granny would boil the water to purify it and then store it in the icebox.

We had no hot tap water. Whenever anyone wanted to take a bath, my parents paid a coolie to carry heavy wooden buckets filled with hot water into our bathroom and empty them into the tub. Sometimes the coolie spilled a little water on the floor, and Granny got angry at him for wasting what we had paid for.

All of our clothes fit into the wardrobe—a tall cabinet with drawers and a small section for hanging garments. We had no closet. Beds were the real problem because they take up so much space. My parents slept in a fold-out bed that became a couch during the day. Granny had a cot that was opened up at bedtime and stored in a corner when not in use. I still slept in my baby crib by the window. Strips of tape crisscrossed the panes to prevent the glass from shattering in case of a bombing. Black drapes kept light from escaping the window at night. During air raids, light could help planes locate their position as they bombed the city. Light could also be mistaken as a possible target. So the drapes helped to protect us.

Despite the small size of our apartment, my parents held parties there. They loved parties, especially my father, who liked to drink with his pals. Eight or nine of their friends somehow fit into the room at the same time. They laughed, told jokes, and just had a good time. I liked these parties, too, because I got to stay up later than usual. But I could never last as long as the grown-ups, and I learned to sleep through anything.

———— * ————

Shanghai was divided into several sections. Foreigners lived and worked in two major areas, the International Settlement and the French Concession, or Frenchtown. These regions were governed by their own laws, separate from Chinese law. This had come about through treaties and agreements signed almost a hundred years earlier by Chinese, British, French, and American officials.

The International Settlement, where we lived, was the largest section. It ran from the western suburbs of the city all the way east to the wharves and docks of the Huangpo River. The French Concession was south of the International Settlement. It also extended west into the suburbs, but it stopped short of the Huangpo River. Although it was called the French Concession, people of many nationalities lived there.

Both my parents' families lived in Shanghai. During the war, though, I saw few relatives on my mother's side. The Japanese had interned most of them in prison camps outside the city. Soon after the Japanese occupied Shanghai in December 1941, they arrested and imprisoned citizens of countries with which they were at war. The Japanese were mostly after the British, but Americans, French, and other Europeans were also interned. My Uncle Jason was left alone because he carried an Iraqi passport. But my Aunt Molly, Cousin Sarah, Uncle Johnny, Cousin Ezra, and some of my mother's other relatives were taken away because they had British passports.

They weren't prisoners exactly because the Japanese didn't lock them up in jail cells behind bars. But they had been forcibly taken away from their homes and families and were held against their will in unpleasant surroundings. Until the war ended three years later, they remained in camp, living under conditions of great hardship and shortage of food.

My parents and my father's family were not interned. They still had their freedom and were able to move around Shanghai as they wished. Because they were either stateless or held Russian passports, the Japanese were not interested in them.

But I was British by birth. One day, when I was only two years old, the Japanese came to our apartment to intern me. Some Japanese guards pounded on the door, demanding, "Where is British subject Gregory Patent?" My frightened parents showed them who I was, proving with my birth certificate that their innocent young child in the crib was the supposed enemy. On learning the truth, the Japanese soldiers started to laugh. My parents could hear them chuckling all the way down the stairs as they left. Suddenly, being British was definitely not the plus factor my parents had expected it to be.

CHAPTER TWO

Wartime Shanghai

✳—————————————✳

B ECAUSE AIR RAIDS were always unpredictable, we had our own drills at the Cosmopolitan Apartments. In the daytime we all ran inside and stayed away from windows when the siren began its long wail. During those at night, my parents covered our window with the blackout curtains and dimmed the light. When the short blasts of the all-clear siren sounded, we resumed whatever we had been doing.

Mostly Russian families lived in the Cosmopolitan Apartments, but the Russian children spoke English when I was around. I understood Russian, the language of my father and his friends, but I never learned to converse in it. I had made up my mind that the only language I'd speak was English.

Even though Shanghai was a victim of war, birthdays were big occasions for celebration in the Russian Jewish community. Since we knew so many families with children, we were invited to parties every five or six weeks.

At some parties the food and drink were lavish, and by the looks of what was on the table, it hardly seemed possible that a war was going on. But in truth, one could get almost anything in Shanghai through something called the black market if one had the money—that was the key.

The black market was the illegal practice of buying or selling things officially restricted or rationed during wartime. But the possibilities for profit were so high that thousands of people risked jail because of it. My parents even tried it once. They bought ten one-hundred-pound sacks of flour when the price was right and stored them on top of the wardrobe. They were waiting for the price of flour to rise before selling. But a few months later, they were horrified to find that the flour sacks were turning green from mildew. In desperation, my father painted the flour sacks white and sold the lot to the first buyer he found. Money was so precious and scarce for my parents that they had to recover what they invested. It was a matter of survival.

Getting enough food was not easy during the war. Only my father worked, and the money he brought in couldn't feed four people. Granny got a small monthly allowance from her son, my uncle Jason. This was pooled with whatever my dad brought in. My parents also had to sell many of their wedding gifts to get money to live on. There came a time when my mother had to part with her engagement and wedding rings in order to buy food. I had never seen her look sadder.

Because I was British but had not been interned, I became eligible to receive food through the Swiss Consulate. Japan was not at war with Switzerland, and the Swiss Consulate handled British affairs in Shanghai during World War II. My mother and I would walk the few blocks from home and line up for the ration, which consisted mostly of cracked wheat, powdered milk, and flour. I was also allowed one loaf of bread each day.

But despite shortages, my parents always made sure I had enough to eat. Sometimes at night my mother cried silent tears of hunger, but I knew nothing of that at the time. While other stomachs were often empty, I was a fussy eater, and it was not always easy to get me to finish what was on my plate. Granny was particularly worried because she thought I was too thin. I often left the table after deciding I'd had enough to eat, and Granny would chase after me with a spoonful of food, saying, "This is for Auntie Molly." After I'd eaten that spoonful, she'd corner me with one morsel after another until I'd eaten for every member of the family except my father. Granny never had me eat for him. For some reason, they didn't get along, and he was left out of this ritual.

Sometimes I'd escape from the apartment to avoid eating, and she'd rush after me down the stairs, shouting, "Gigi, you must eat your food." Once outside, I'd scramble through a hole in a nearby fence to another apartment building where she couldn't find me. It was a battle of wills, and we both won our share over time.

Rats needed food, too. They were bold animals. One morning I found large holes in a pair of socks I hadn't put away the night before. That's how we knew we had unwanted guests. We searched everywhere for weeks without finding where they were living. Then one morning Granny discovered their nest while cleaning the bathroom. The rats had been hiding in a corner under the bathtub that was hard to reach. She killed them all on the spot with a broom. We never had rats again after that.

Cockroaches also made their home with us. But they weren't a serious nuisance, and we'd only catch them by surprise. Coming home at night to a dark apartment and turning on the light, we'd see the large brown insects scurrying in every direction and disappearing as if by a magician's trick. My mother always shuddered at the sight of them. I'm not sure why, but I secretly liked the cockroaches.

Every few months, whenever they got to be more than my parents or Granny could bear, my father bought a smoke bomb, which flushed out the cockroaches and killed them. We couldn't stay at home during this process and usually visited Uncle Jason and his family in the western suburbs of the city.

Uncle Jason, his wife, Mosel, and their three daughters lived in a huge home surrounded by lots of grass and trees. My cousins, Esther, Rachma, and Florrie, were older than I, but all the same we had fun playing together. A swing, hanging from one of the tall trees, was the best part. We took turns pushing each other, but since I was the youngest and smallest, I pushed the least and was pushed the most.

Uncle Jason's home was so big I sometimes got lost in it. In 1935, on the night of my parents' wedding, Uncle Jason and his wife had hosted a sit-down dinner for a hundred and fifty people! There were many such mansions in Shanghai, owned by wealthy Chinese and foreigners alike.

———— * ————

I spent lots of time with my mother during the war. I felt safe when I was with her. She had been a file clerk and secretary for an American company, but with the Japanese takeover, she was out of a job. She showed me how to read, helping me pronounce words properly and teaching me new ones. We read together often. She wanted to be sure I learned to speak like a Britisher, so we worked on that a lot.

She also taught me numbers and how to tell time. In the mornings I went to the Jewish school, a few blocks up Seymour Road. I was in kindergarten and played games most of the time. Granny or

my mother walked me there and came to pick me up at noon. After lunch my mother and I normally spent our time quietly reading, exploring the city, or roaming through parks. Another apartment complex, the Garden Apartments, was a short walk from home. My mother would take me there often so that I could play with the children and she could chat with her friends. Air raids sometimes changed our plans, but we adjusted our lives to them.

Sometimes we'd make an excursion to Jessfield Park, several miles to the west, near the outskirts of

Shanghai. I loved running on the grassy lawns and watching the graceful ducks and swans swimming and diving for food in the ponds. Because the park was so far away, we'd take either a rickshaw or a pedicab—a wheeled carriage pulled by a driver on a bicycle—to get there. Money was usually too short to spend on nonessentials, so these were special trips.

Riding in a rickshaw was always an adventure. My mother bargained with the coolie, gesturing with her hands to settle on a fare before we started off. I learned all the hand signals for Chinese numbers and used them myself when I was older and traveled in the city alone. After agreeing on a price, we'd both squeeze into the narrow seat and be ready to head off. The coolie picked up the front end of the rickshaw and started to run with the traffic. Rickshaw coolies worked very hard and for little pay. Some were too poor to afford shoes.

The congested streets in Shanghai made any kind of travel hazardous. Rickshaw coolies, pedicab drivers, and bicyclists all tried to deny the existence of each other and of cars. In addition, the streets were flooded with automobiles, tooting and beeping their horns without stopping. Buses, trucks, and streetcars added to the never-ending noise.

Pedestrians often wandered into our path, and the coolie would veer the rickshaw instantly to avoid accidents. But several people a day died on the streets of Shanghai, usually victims of cars or trucks.

Beggars of all ages, some horribly maimed or deformed, were everywhere. Occasionally a young beggar ran right alongside us with outstretched hands, sometimes for a few blocks, pleading in broken English for some change: "No mama, no papa—you give money?" Coolies hauled baskets heavy with food or merchandise, supported by a bamboo pole slung over their shoulders. They trudged along the roadside, each step accompanied by a rhythmic up-and-down swaying of their burden.

———— * ————

While my mother and I were out and about—to the extent that air raids allowed us—Granny spent most of her time at home. She did all the cooking. Her fragrant, delicious dishes taught me to love Middle Eastern food. When we could afford it, she baked crisp, ring-shaped cookies called *kakas* or others called *milfoof,* crunchy rolls of pastry with walnuts, sugar, and cinnamon. I loved their names, but I loved munching them even more. Our apartment always had wonderful smells from Granny's cooking.

Sometimes I went shopping with Granny at the Seymour Road Market, across Bubbling Well Road. It was a huge indoor store with all kinds of food for sale. Vendors there sold fresh vegetables, fruit, live chickens, ducks, geese, and even live fish swimming in tanks. Granny bought a chicken from one man and took it over to Uncle Shaul's stall to be killed the kosher way. Uncle Shaul was a distant relative of ours and a butcher by trade. He sold beef and lamb, but not chickens. Uncle Shaul twirled the chicken by its neck over his head a few times while saying some sort of prayer. Then he cut the chicken's throat and let it bleed to death in a large barrel. That was the kosher way of killing. It may seem cruel, but the chicken died very quickly. If you didn't care about the food being kosher, the vendors would kill what you bought.

But many Chinese preferred to take live chickens and fish home with them to be killed there. They'd carry chickens by their feet or tie them to their bicycles for the ride home. Many residences had outdoor sinks, and I often saw people killing and cleaning poultry or fish right outside their front doors.

Foreigners in Shanghai employed amahs— Chinese women who washed clothes, cleaned the house, or took care of children. Since my mother didn't work, I had no amah then, but the family hired one to wash our clothes. Even though money was tight for us and for other foreigners, we always seemed better off than most Chinese. Chinese workers lived in very cramped quarters. Sometimes as many as ten people, from two or three different families, could be crowded into a single room the same size as ours. Usually there was no indoor plumbing or heating.

All through the war, Dad worked as an announcer for radio station XMHA. It didn't pay much, but the work was steady. I listened to my father's program a lot because he played my favorite music. All of it was from 1941 or earlier because no new records came into Shanghai during the war. Bing Crobsy and Dinah Shore were the singers I liked most. I'd listen to her version of "Smoke Gets in Your Eyes" over and over again. But perhaps the song I liked best was Carmen Miranda's "South American Way." Her foreign accent intrigued me. And every time I heard the wonderful way she sang the word *south*—she made it sound like "souse"—I'd giggle with delight.

Dad even got me to perform on the radio. I made my debut one afternoon singing "Somewhere Over the Rainbow." He was in the control room, while I was in the studio standing on a chair so that I could reach the microphone. I started to sing the first line. Then, just to make sure I could be heard, I shouted into the microphone, "Can you hear me, Daddy, can you hear me?" to the amusement of every listener in Shanghai.

We owned an old phonograph—one of those that you had to crank up—and a sizable collection of records. Dad would bring home some that were too worn out to play on the radio, but they sounded just fine to me on our machine. Once he surprised my mother with an anniversary gift of his own recording of "Let Me Call You Sweetheart." She played it over and over, and I can still hear his voice singing the words as if the song had been written just for her.

Things weren't always so happy at home, though. My father was often away in the evenings and didn't come home until quite late. Once or twice I was frightened when angry voices woke me from my sleep, but I never knew what the problem was. My father had a violent temper and often got angry for no apparent reason. On occasion, he would hit me, and I never knew why.

CHAPTER THREE

Friends
My Own Age

————————————

MY BEST FRIEND at the Cosmopolitan Apartments was Dolly Braude. She was a year younger than I and lived in the apartment right above us on the top floor of the building. Dolly was my first girl friend. She had light brown curly hair, a beautiful smile, and a twinkle in her eyes. We spent many hours together walking, sharing secrets, and playing games. If either of us had any problems, we tried to comfort each other. I had even made up my mind to marry her after we grew up.

In the fall of 1944, I got the measles. The light in the room was an eerie red during the day because my parents hung red covers on the window to keep the room darkened. Too strong a light was thought to damage the eyes of someone with measles.

Dolly's mother wanted Dolly to catch the disease because every child was expected to come down with it, and the sooner the better. So she sent Dolly downstairs to be with me as much as possible while

I was ill. Dolly never did catch the measles from me, but playing with her helped to relieve my boredom. Being cooped up in a crib for several days was no fun.

About this time I also discovered I had a case of worms. One morning, soon after waking, I sneezed, and out of my nose came a white, wriggling worm about the size of a pencil. I screamed in terror as the worm thrashed on the floor. My mother cradled me in her arms while my father flushed the ugly thing down the toilet. "It's all right, Gigi, dear," my mother said. "You've got worms. Everybody gets them, and there's nothing to worry about. Even Dolly's had worms. There's medicine the doctor will give you to get rid of them." You mean there might be more of them living inside me? I thought. Fortunately, no more worms came out of me while I was being treated, and within a few weeks the doctor said I was cured. But I was afraid to sneeze for a long time after that.

In early 1945, a few months after recovering from these infections, I came down with whooping cough. It was miserable not only for me but also for my mother, who developed a case at the same time. But at least I didn't have to stay in bed. We coughed together and complained to each other about how much our chests hurt. Even though I had her company, it was a lonely time. Because the disease was so contagious, we couldn't visit friends. Fortunately, the spring weather was warm, and we'd go up to the roof garden on top of our building to take sunbaths and try to bake away the illness. Sometimes we heard antiaircraft gunfire off in the distance, but it was too far away to do us any harm.

The whooping cough finally left us, but my mother came down with something else. She got sick almost every morning and sometimes in the evenings. She seemed even thinner than usual. A doctor came to our apartment one day to examine her, and I was not allowed to stay in the room. I waited on the landing outside the door, pacing back and forth, and imagined all sorts of diseases my mother could have. Finally I was allowed back in. My mother saw the worry in my eyes and hugged me close to her.

She said, "Gigi, darling, there's nothing to be upset about." Then she looked at me and said, "The doctor's just told me that I'm going to have a baby."

I didn't know what to think.

"Really, Mummy?" I asked. "When? How soon?" I pretended to be excited by the news.

"In about six months. The doctor says late November."

I was relieved, even grateful, that my mother wasn't really sick. But did I want a brother or sister? I liked being the only child. I didn't know if I wanted to share my parents and Granny with anyone else.

My mother's tummy gradually grew bigger as the weather got hotter. She still got sick, but now I knew what was causing it.

The war finally ended in the summer of 1945. The United States dropped two atomic bombs on Japan in August, and within a few days the Japanese surrendered.

More and more low-flying American planes now roared across the Shanghai skies. The silvery B-29s were the most impressive. They seemed unbelievably big and powerful to me. Now that the war was over, they weren't dropping bombs. They were distributing much-needed relief supplies by parachute. The American food they dropped looked strange to us at first. But we were hungry, and I remember eating a spicy canned meat called Spam for the first time and loving it. The brightly colored parachutes floating slowly to earth were signs that peace at last had come to Shanghai.

———— * ————

The reclaiming of Shanghai by the Chinese in August 1945 went smoothly. The Japanese surrendered, and life gradually returned to normal. The best thing about the war's end was that there were no more air raids or bombings to worry about. My mother couldn't go back to work yet because she suffered from morning sickness that seemed to go on all day. There was still a housing shortage, so we stayed on with Granny. My father no longer

worked for the radio station. He had a better paying job with an appliance firm. But money was still in short supply since only he worked.

All our relatives who had been interned by the Japanese during the war were released, and I was very happy to be with them again. But it shocked me to see how thin they looked. I was especially glad to be with Auntie Molly, one of my mother's sisters. She had always pampered me before the war. She loved to give me baths and generally spoiled me. My cousins, Sarah and Ezra, Molly's children, were in their teens and had also endured the war in prison camp. Ezra, who was not feeling well, stayed with us for a few days while he waited for housing to be found for himself, Sarah, and Molly. Somehow we made room for him in our small apartment. Uncle Johnny went back to live with his mother, my Aunt Sally.

Despite housing shortages, money could get you anything, and my Uncle Jason had money. His wife's family was wealthy and owned a large building on the corner of Bubbling Well Road and Seymour Road, just a block away from us. Auntie Molly and her children moved into an apartment there. Because they lived so close, we saw each other often.

Ezra soon left for England to see some doctors. In camp he had come down with a strange disease called dropsy, which made him swell up and look very puffy. The doctors in Shanghai didn't know how to treat it, so they arranged for Ezra to see specialists in London. I felt so sorry for him—all those years in a prison camp and now this sickness. Shortly after arriving in England, Ezra died. Aunt Molly and Sarah were heartbroken. Ezra was the first person I knew who had died.

During September of 1945, more and more foreigners came to Shanghai. Several families moved into the Cosmopolitan Apartments, including Europeans, Filipinos, and Americans. I made friends with an eight-year-old Swedish girl named Teddy. She loved to play all sorts of games. Dolly played with us, too, of course. Eding and Joey, a sister and brother, were my new Filipino playmates. She was about seven, and he was five. Everyone spoke English, so communicating was easy.

Hide-and-go-seek was one of our favorite games because there were so many terrific hiding places in the Cosmopolitan Apartments. Several buildings made up the apartment complex. The main building—the tallest one—was in the center, with a large courtyard in front of it. Only rich people lived there. Cars, rickshaws, and pedicabs were usually parked out front. Off to the sides were several three- or four-story buildings where people with less money lived. Long alleyways, doorways, and various nooks and crannies throughout the area made ideal hiding places.

"Home" was usually the front steps of the main building. Whoever was "it" would hide his head and count while the rest of us scattered to our hiding places. "Ready or not, here I come" was our signal to stay as hidden as possible. If we tagged home before we were discovered, we were safe.

One evening I was "it." It was after dark, and I had found everybody except Teddy. We were all puzzled as to where she might be. I was deciding where to search next when an old Chinese woman, whose feet had been bound years earlier, hobbled slowly with the aid of a cane into the courtyard and toward the main steps. Women like her were common in Shanghai, and I always felt sorry for them. The custom of foot-binding originated in ancient China because men thought women looked prettier with tiny feet, and a woman with bound feet couldn't easily leave home. A girl's feet were wrapped tightly with bandages when she was very young in order to prevent her feet from growing. It caused lifelong pain and discomfort, and the practice was eventually outlawed.

"I'm safe!" said the old Chinese woman. I was dumbstruck. It was Teddy in disguise.

"What? How did you do it?" I asked stupidly.

"I just happened to find this stick while I was looking for a place to hide, and that gave me the idea," she said proudly. "All I did was use my sweater as a shawl, hunch my back a little, and walk slowly."

All the kids started telling her how clever she was to think of a stunt like that, and I marveled at her ingenuity. She had made her way all across the courtyard and up the steps in plain view, and none of us suspected there was anything odd.

———— * ————

In late September my mother, who was seven months pregnant, had an offer of a secretarial job. Since she was finally feeling better, she took it. The extra money would come in handy for the baby. It was also time for me to go back to school and for Dolly to start. We both went to the Jewish school in the mornings and played with friends in the afternoons and evenings. Fall evenings were cool and very pleasant out of doors. I played outside to get away from our stuffy apartment and to keep out of my father's way. He seemed angry at me a lot lately. I became afraid of him and tried my best not to upset him.

Since so much of our time was spent in the courtyard, we saw everyone who resided in the apartments as they came or went. One woman who lived on the top floor of the main building had her own chauffeur, which was common in Shanghai if you were rich. We were curious about her because she always wore black clothes, never said hello to us children, and seemed very mysterious. If we happened to be playing on the steps when she left the building or came home, we quietly moved out of the way to let her pass.

"I hear she's a witch," a boy named Moses Eskin whispered to me one day.

Witch? I thought to myself. He must be wrong. Witches don't really exist except in fairy tales.

"How do you know?" I asked.

"I've heard this from other people," he said knowingly. "They say she eats strange things."

I didn't know what to make of all this. Moses might well be making it up, I thought. But he did live in the same building as the woman, and he would know if the rumor was true. We were all afraid of witches, and we didn't want one living among us.

One night while we were playing in the court-yard, Teddy suggested we try to scare the woman. The plan was for Moses, Dolly, Teddy, Eding, Joey, and me to climb the stairs to her apartment, ring the bell, and then run away. When she answered the door and found nobody there, that would frighten her. I don't think any of us really thought this bit of business would scare a real witch. But doing it became a test of our own courage.

It was very dark climbing the eight flights of stairs, and we could barely see our way. People always used the elevator, so there were no lights in the stairway. We didn't dare take the elevator, though, because the operator would wonder what we were all up to. We went slowly in order not to trip, each of us holding on to another. We whispered, trying to reassure ourselves that we weren't afraid. On the last flight of stairs I felt something brush my face.

"It's a ghost!" I screamed and raced blindly down the stairs, holding on to the railing for dear life. Then everyone panicked, running, yelling, and screaming behind me. Once outside the building, we gasped for air. I could feel my heart pounding in my chest.

"It was a ghost. A ghost touched my face. I swear it was a ghost," I said. "Didn't any of you feel it?"

"It wasn't a ghost. It was me," said Teddy, smiling.

"You? Why? What did you do that for?"

"Just to see what would happen," she said.

By then the other kids had caught their breath and started laughing.

"I don't see what's so funny. We were going to scare a witch, and now you've spoiled it," I yelled at Teddy.

They kept laughing, which only upset me more and made me angrier. Then Dolly tried to calm me down. She said Teddy didn't mean any harm, that we all had fun on this adventure, and that my reaction made it all the more exciting.

Well, I had to admit it was exciting. And I marveled again at Teddy's cleverness.

CHAPTER FOUR

My Sunday
with George

* ———————————————— *

B Y LATE OCTOBER 1945, Americans were again
part of life in Shanghai. American businesses
that were closed during the war reopened their
doors. Military men stationed in the Pacific also
came to enjoy the entertainment and night life the
city was famous for.

The YMCA served as a social center for new
American arrivals, whether they were in port for
a few days or had come to settle. It had a library,
bowling alley, swimming pool, basketball courts,
and all sorts of exercise equipment. My father
often bowled there on weekends and got to meet
many Americans.

One was George, a major in the American Army.
He had a family in the United States and a son about
my age. He was feeling homesick, so my father
invited him over to our apartment one evening to
have a drink and to meet my mother, Granny, and
me. George and I took an instant liking to each

other. He was dressed in uniform, which impressed me very much. We were all chatting when George asked if I'd like to spend a day going around the city with him. I eagerly looked over at my mother and father, and when they saw how much I liked the idea, they gave their approval. George arranged a time to pick me up the next day and returned to his hotel. I had never gone out with someone I hardly knew, but I was very excited.

It was Sunday. My mother dressed me all in white—shirt, shorts, shoes, and socks. Her tummy was quite big now, for it would be only about a month before she had the baby.

George arrived a little before noon. He assured my parents and Granny that he would take very good care of me, and off we went. The weather was perfect—sunny and warm with a slight breeze. He hired a pedicab in the courtyard to take us downtown. I knew how much it should cost, since I'd made the trip many times with my mother, so I helped George bargain with the coolie. Since George was a stranger to Shanghai, I was going to act as his guide.

Turning left onto the street put us on Seymour Road. The sidewalks were narrow, and the street itself was crowded with rickshaws, pedicabs, bicyclists, and noisy automobiles. Beggars, as usual, were everywhere. But this was true of almost any street in Shanghai.

We soon reached Bubbling Well Road. This was

one of the major thoroughfares in Shanghai. It ran for miles and was well known for its shops. I always loved the name of this street. At one time there had been a well where the streetcar made its turnaround a few miles to the west, but now the well was dry. We turned east and headed toward downtown.

At major intersections, policemen in small cubicles raised a few feet above the street, called kiosks, tried to control the traffic. But despite their efforts, there was always confusion in the streets. George just shook his head and wondered why there weren't accidents all the time. He said that in America people actually obeyed traffic signals. I was amazed, unable to imagine what that must be like.

Most of the buildings in this part of town were a few stories high. It was only when we got closer to downtown that tall hotels, shops, and office buildings appeared. But even so, Shanghai did not have any real skyscrapers. The highest building was only about twenty stories.

We got the pedicab driver to let us off at the imposing Park Hotel, one of my favorites among Shanghai's taller buildings. In sunlight it had a deep purple color. It was right next door to the YMCA. Up the street a short way was the Grand Cinema, one of the biggest movie theatres in the world, I was told.

George took me to lunch at the Park Hotel, high up on one of the top floors. The ride in the elevator was thrilling, as I had never gone up so many stories before. The dining room was very large, with high ceilings and wide marble windowsills. A well-dressed Chinese waiter seated us and presented menus. I had never eaten in such a fancy place, and I was a bit confused. Although I could read well, I had never had to choose what I ate before, and there were so many different things on the menu.

"Well, Greg, what are you in the mood for?" George asked.

I wasn't used to being called Greg, and so I asked him to please call me Gigi. He said he would if I'd call him George. Up to then I had addressed him as Major. I never called adults by their first names, and it made me uncomfortable. But George explained that in America it was common for children to use the first names of adults. So, wanting to please him, I did. Once that was settled, I told him that I liked almost anything.

"Well, is it O.K. with you if I order chicken for both of us? Do you like chicken?"

"Yes, chicken will be fine," I said. But I didn't know what O.K. meant. So I asked him. That was the first American expression I learned. I taught it to my friends later, and we all used it regularly.

During lunch we talked about George's life in the Army and my life in Shanghai. He also told me of his family in America and how he was looking forward to being with them again soon. He'd been away from home for several months now. He showed me snapshots of his wife and children, and I pictured myself posing with them. What would it be like to visit America? I wondered. How would it be to have George for a father?

After the delicious lunch, we got into another pedicab and continued on toward the heart of the city. To add to the confusion caused by so much traffic, many streets in Shanghai changed names at certain places. Bubbling Well Road became Nanking Road downtown, but it was really the same street.

Our pedicab approached the Bund, the Shanghai waterfront, where all the ships docked. On our left was the magnificent Cathay Hotel. It wasn't as tall as the Park Hotel, but its top was shaped like a pyramid with four sides, and I loved to look at it. The appliance store where my father worked was in the hotel's arcade. Across the street stood the Palace Hotel. Its rich red brick made it stand out from the dull gray buildings around it. The Palace was a favorite eating place of business people. In Shanghai, office workers had two-hour lunches, so they could enjoy relaxing meals without worrying about time.

We had the pedicab driver drop us off at the Bund. I loved being on the Bund. It was my favorite place in all Shanghai. It bustled with activity, both on land and on the water. Strolling along the wide sidewalk by the Huangpo River, I tried to imagine what it would be like to actually take a trip on a ship. My parents told me some Chinese spent their entire lives

on the water, in boats called sampans and junks. I couldn't imagine what that would be like—never setting foot on land or going for walks, always cooped up with nowhere else to go.

Across the wide river from the Bund was an area with factories and warehouses known as Pootung. Uncle Boris, my father's brother-in-law, worked in a feather-processing plant there, and Pootung became his nickname.

"Gigi, how'd you like to go on the river?"

"You mean on a boat?"

"Yes, of course," George said, chuckling. "We can rent a launch and take a short trip."

"Oh, that would be wonderful," I said.

George bargained with the pilot and helped me down the steps and onto the launch, a small, open boat with a few seats. Getting a foothold was a bit tricky because the launch bobbed up and down in the water. We sat down and sped off toward Pootung. The spray from the water felt refreshing. About halfway there, in the middle of the river, the launch slowed down and turned to face the Bund.

I looked back to where we'd been and had my first view of the Bund from the water. What a sight! All my favorite buildings, a mixture of European and Oriental architecture, were laid out in front of me: the Customs House with its marvelous clock tower; the Shanghai Club, a beautiful white building with tall columns and a huge dome; the Bank of China; and the Palace and Cathay Hotels.

George asked me how I liked it so far, and I really couldn't say much. Everything was so breathtaking. The launch went all along the Bund, from one end to the other, and I did my best to absorb it all. After we docked, I felt a bit shaky, so we went for a walk in the park at the end of the Bund.

"Are you O.K., Gigi?"

"Yes, George, I'm really fine, just excited."

For a final treat, George bought me a huge dish of ice cream at the Palace Hotel. I forced myself to eat it all, not caring if I got sick later. To top things off, we stopped at the downtown PX, a store open only to employees of the American government, and George picked up some candy bars for me to take home. I was in heaven. One candy bar was named E-Z Bite, which puzzled me. The *Z* in British English is pronounced "zed," and I had no idea what E-Zed was supposed to mean. When George explained that in America *Z* is pronounced "zee," the name made perfect sense, and I had a good laugh over it.

I knew the day was coming to an end, but I wasn't prepared for my reaction. George brought me home after dark, and on the way back in the pedicab I was dreading the fact that we had to part. I liked being with him so much that I wished he didn't have to leave. He walked me up the stairs to our apartment and came inside for a few minutes. My father was out, but my mother and Granny were there to greet us. George thanked my mother for allowing me to go out with him, and then he hugged me and told me how much fun he had had. I couldn't speak. Then he left.

I burst into tears. No matter what my mother said or did, I couldn't be comforted. Mother and Granny didn't know what to make of my behavior. They kept asking me what was wrong, and I couldn't answer them. I had spent this perfectly wonderful day, and here I was behaving as though I'd been mistreated. No one could understand my misery.

The truly special thing about my time with George was that I could be myself. He liked me for who I was, not for how he wanted me to behave. He was a military man, yet he was gentle. My father was not like that. Although I knew he loved me, and he did nice things for me, it was hard to be natural with him. He was gruff by nature, and his behavior was unpredictable. I never knew where I stood or how he might react, so I was always on guard.

George, on the other hand, seemed to care about me and my feelings. I hardly knew him, and yet his kindness made me trust him. It was as if we were equals on one level. Were all American men like George? I wondered.

Whether they were or not, from then on I desperately wished things could be like that with my own father.

CHAPTER FIVE

Movies, Bobby, and Baba

* ———————————— *

ABOUT A WEEK after my outing with George, my mother said she had a surprise for me. "Gigi, dear, how would you like to see the film *Snow White?*" I had never been to a movie, and I couldn't wait to go.

My parents had seen many American films, and they had tried to describe what the experience was like. But I couldn't imagine a picture being as large as they said it would be, or that it would move. Up to now I had had to make up pictures in my own mind whenever I listened to the radio or read a story. Television, of course, wasn't even available yet.

In Shanghai movie theatres, all seats were reserved, so my mother bought tickets in advance for a Saturday matinee. The lobby of the Cathay Theatre was huge, with several large chandeliers hanging down from the high ceiling. An usher wearing a strange-looking uniform showed us to our seats on the main floor. Looking around the large auditorium, I noticed people sitting upstairs in the balcony. Soon after, the lights dimmed, and the movie began.

I was immediately transported into the world of film. At first I had a hard time believing what I was seeing. The giant screen was filled with color, motion, and sound; and the cartoon characters actually spoke English! Despite the newness of the experience, I got into the story fast. I became afraid when Snow White was sent into the woods all alone, and the evil queen gave me a few uneasy moments. But I loved all the songs and sang many of them to myself later. In order for the Chinese people to understand what was going on, there were panels on each side of the screen for subtitles. Since Chinese is written in vertical columns, the panels were tall and narrow.

One film and I was hooked forever! I had so much fun I asked my mother if we could please see another one soon. Because the baby was getting pretty big, she found it uncomfortable to sit for very long in one position, but she took me anyway the next weekend. This time we went to see *Dumbo*. I was completely engrossed in the story and felt very sorry for Dumbo because all the other elephants and children made fun of his huge ears. When Dumbo's mother was taken off to jail for defending him, I cried out loud. What if my mother were taken away from me like that? I became so upset that my mother had to take me into the lobby until I calmed down.

"Gigi, darling, don't cry. It's only a movie," she said.

"No, it's not," I sobbed. "They took Dumbo's mummy away from him." By now I was wailing.

"I'm sure everything will turn out all right in the end, Gigi," she said, stroking my hair. Some of the theatre attendants gathered around us, wondering what was wrong. My mother assured them everything would be all right soon. In a few minutes I calmed down. "Do you want to go back in and see the rest of the movie, Gigi?"

I began thinking about the colorful circus scenes and decided to see the rest of *Dumbo*. We went back to our seats, and in a little while I started to enjoy the movie again. My mother was right; the film did have a happy ending. But even after I left the theatre, I kept feeling sad for Dumbo. The fact that his mother had been taken away from him kept bothering me for a long time. What if the same thing happened to me?

———— * ————

November was rainy and cold. My mother woke up late one night with labor pains and asked to go to the hospital. My father was not with us because he had done something to make Granny angry, and she had kicked him out of the apartment a few days earlier. Granny went upstairs to wake Dolly's mother, Fanny Braude, and she took my mother to the hospital. Fanny returned the next morning looking very happy. She announced that my mother was fine and that she had given birth to a healthy baby boy.

A few days later my father came home with my mother and my new baby brother, Bobby. I was very curious about Bobby, but I got angry with him almost as soon as they brought him into the apartment. After proudly showing him to me and to Granny, my mother set him down in my crib! I protested loudly. Then Mother explained.

"It's his crib now, Gigi. You're a big boy and can sleep in a real bed," she told me. But I loved my cozy crib, where I'd slept all my life. It was the one part of the little room that was all mine, and I didn't want to give it up. That same day my father bought me a chair that opened up into a bed and squeezed it into a small space by the window. I didn't like it at all. It wasn't really mine, like the crib had been. Anyone could sit there during the daytime. It only belonged to me at night.

I looked down at my brother lying in the crib. His big, dark eyes in a fat, round face were gazing unsteadily at me. I hated him. I thought to myself, I'd like to throw him out the window. *Jealousy* was a word I had heard others use, but now I knew what it meant.

The first few weeks Bobby was home, I

pretended that I liked and loved him. But what I really felt was that he had taken over. Don't do this or that, I was told; you'll disturb the baby. Gigi, you must be quiet; the baby's sleeping. All our relatives came over to ooh and ah over him. Bobby looked so sweet nursing at my mother's breast, and she seemed delighted to have him there. And I felt rage that I'd been replaced.

———— * ————

In December, the Jewish holiday of Hanukkah helped to take my mind off Bobby. Hanukkah serves as a reminder of religious freedom for the Jews. The most memorable part of Hanukkah was the lighting of the eight lamps, one for each night of the holiday. For Jews from Eastern Europe, it was the custom to use a special candle holder called a menorah for this ritual. But in Iraq Granny learned to burn oil lamps for Hanukkah. She continued the practice in Shanghai, making them in her own way. First she fashioned wicks several inches long out of bamboo. She shaved bamboo with a knife into slivers and then wrapped them with cotton. Once the wicks were made, she attached each one to a flat metal base. For each lamp she put water into a special glass used only for this purpose. Granny floated a layer of oil on top of the water. Then she carefully placed a mounted wick in the oil, the metal base resting on the bottom of the glass with the tip of the stiff bamboo wick extending up from the oil layer. She put the most oil into the first two or three lamps, since they had to burn the longest.

On the first day of Hanukkah, she lit two lamps at sunset. The first lamp was called the shammes, or helper lamp, used to light all the others. The second lamp signified the first night of Hanukkah. Granny recited a prayer before and after the kindling. She spoke softly and with great seriousness. Granny repeated this ceremony for seven more nights, using the shammes lamp to light each subsequent one. By the end of Hanukkah, there were nine lamps burning, giving our small apartment a warm golden glow.

The fun part of Hanukkah was playing with a special top called a dreidel. It has four sides, each with a different Hebrew letter, and the bottom comes to a point, on which it turns. You spin the dreidel by twirling a small knob on its top. We children sometimes used the dreidel in a game of gambling. It made us feel like grown-ups. Whether you won or lost depended on which letter came up after the dreidel finished spinning and came to rest. I used the small change my parents and relatives gave me as Hanukkah presents to gamble with Dolly and some of my other Jewish friends. Of course, I loved winning. But I gambled for the excitement of it more than anything else.

———— * ————

Baba, my father's mother, also lived in Shanghai. She was an exceptional cook and baker and often brought over special treats for us, especially during Hanukkah and other Jewish holidays. Baba was famous for her Napoleons—crispy layers of flaky, buttery pastry filled with a creamy custard. Each Napoleon was rectangular in shape, and the top was dusted with powdered sugar. They were beautiful and delicious. I usually ate them by hand, stuffing as much as I could into my mouth at one time. They went down quicker that way than with a fork.

Baba was so good at baking that she made a small business out of it. Friends would pay her to make Napoleons and other pastries. She lived in an apartment in the French Concession, on Avenue Joffre, about fifteen minutes away from us by pedicab. When she brought us pastries, she packed them carefully in a box and carried them on her lap so they'd arrive in perfect condition. Sometimes she brought us real food, too, such as *pilmeni*, delicious Russian raviolis she made by hand.

Baba was very different from Granny. She was taller and seemed stern and was always very formal. She stood very straight, with square shoulders, and she had the most beautiful white hair. Baba loved me and was affectionate with me, but in a reserved way. I didn't get the kind of big hugs from her that Granny gave me so freely. I loved Baba, too. But I knew that I could only get so close and no closer, so I usually felt uneasy when I was with her.

Baba had become a widow about two months before my parents' wedding. After my parents married, both Baba and Granny lived with them for a while in a large rented house. But this soon proved to be an impossible situation. The two older women couldn't speak the same language, and both wanted to run the kitchen and the household. Each night when my parents came home from work, Granny complained in Arabic to my mother about her horrible day with Baba, and Baba lamented about Granny in Russian to my father. This went on for a few months until finally nobody could stand it any longer. Granny moved into the Cosmopolitan Apartments alone. Baba moved in with her daughter, my aunt Luba. My parents moved into a boarding house.

During the war, when my parents couldn't afford to buy enough food, Baba made a special concoction for my mother, who was painfully thin. She cooked lard with chopped apples until all the water was evaporated and gave it to my mother to spread on bread, as though it were butter. Ordinarily, Granny wouldn't allow any pork product in our house because she kept a strictly kosher kitchen. But she worried about my mother's health and made an exception. My mother didn't particularly like the lard, but she ate it because sometimes that's all there was.

Baba knew some Russian folk medicine, too. January and February 1946 were particularly damp and cold, and my father suffered several bad asthma attacks. When he was ill, Baba came over and treated him in a special way, which always fascinated me.

She held a lighted match inside a heavy water glass turned upside down to burn off any oxygen. Then she pressed the mouth of the glass onto my father's chest, where it created a vacuum, sucking up a lump of his flesh. She repeated this procedure with many glasses, until my father's chest was covered with rows and rows of glasses.

As the vacuums broke, Baba removed the glasses one by one. My father's chest was covered with red circles, looking as though he had been attacked by a giant octopus. My father then turned over and lay on his stomach, and Baba applied the glasses to his back in the same way. I think the idea behind this treatment was that the suction would draw the agent causing the asthma out of his body. Whatever the theory, the method appeared to work, since my father was able to breathe again without wheezing.

———— * ————

The wet and cold of winter dragged on into March, and I found it increasingly crowded in our small apartment. I welcomed being at school during the mornings, but the weather usually kept me from playing outside in the afternoons. I was getting used to Bobby now, realizing he was not going to go away. I spent a lot of my time haunting the Uptown Theatre on the corner of Bubbling Well Road and Seymour Road, just up the street. All my spare money went to pay for movies, and when I didn't have any, the cashier would let me sneak in after the feature started. I saw *Pinocchio* eight times that way. Often I'd just stand in the lobby and listen to the sound track filtering its way through the doors. Tarzan's movies impressed me the most. He was strong, yet gentle. I loved watching him swing through the trees, and I wished I could play the part of Boy. I wanted to be in movies, too, because they were magic to me.

Seeing so many American movies made me continue to wonder what it would be like living in America. On one of my visits to the theatre, I saw a street vendor near the entrance selling something called bubble gum. It was made in America, and I'd never seen anything like it before. He was chewing it and blowing bubbles to advertise the product, and I stared at him as though he were the greatest trickster in the world. I just had to have some, but I didn't have any money. I ran home and told Granny excitedly about bubble gum and asked her if she'd please let me have the money to buy it.

"No, Gigi," she said, "gum not good for teeth."

Teeth! I thought. Who cares about teeth?

I pleaded and pleaded, describing to her what the man was able to do with the gum, but it was useless.

She wasn't going to let me have the money. Then, when she turned to attend to a pot on the stove, I did it. In a split second I opened her purse, reached in, pulled out the money I needed, and was out of the apartment. With luck, she wouldn't miss the paltry sum.

I ran back to the vendor, handed him the stolen money, and bought the package of gum. He spoke broken English, and I asked him to please show me how to blow bubbles. I watched him carefully, imitating his movements with my gum. Slowly I got the hang of it, and I left to practice on my own for about an hour. Bubble gum was magic; how else to explain it? When I got tired of chewing, I wadded the gum up into a ball and stuck it behind my left ear, a trick George had showed me when he chewed ordinary gum. That way the gum was there when I wanted it again.

When I got back home, I hid the remaining pieces of gum in some clothing. I felt terrible guilt for what I'd done, stealing from Granny like that. I'd never stolen anything before. And from Granny? But then I thought about all the gum I had left and how much fun I'd have chewing it, and the guilt vanished. When I got my own money, I'd buy more gum, and then I'd be able to show Granny and my parents what wondrous things I could do with bubble gum.

CHAPTER SIX

Good-bye, Joey

———————————

MY MOTHER WENT BACK to work again shortly before Passover, about the middle of March. My parents hired an amah, Lindy, to take care of Bobby during the day and do the laundry. I spent less time with my mother because she didn't come home until dinner time. But now that the weather was warming up, I played outdoors with my friends or went to the Uptown Theatre. More and more American films were opening in Shanghai, and I wanted to see them all.

We usually went to Uncle Shaul's house for the seder meals, which were held the first two nights of the week-long Passover observance. He and his wife and five children lived in a large home along the lane leading into the Cosmopolitan Apartments.

About a week after Passover, it was time for Russian Easter. We didn't observe Easter because we were Jewish. But most of my father's friends weren't, and to them Easter was the most important

Russian celebration of the year, even more important than Christmas. On Easter Sunday my father and I dressed up and went all over Shanghai by pedicab or streetcar to visit the homes of several of our friends. It was the custom for the women to stay home while the men did the visiting. I loved going out with my father during Easter because it was just the two of us, and I hardly ever spent any time with him alone.

Grown-ups at these gatherings drank lots of ice-cold vodka, but they always ate a bite of food after downing each gulp.

"That way we don't get drunk," my father explained.

I celebrated my seventh birthday in May 1946. Our next-door neighbor, Mrs. Tuchinsky, had a large four-room apartment, and she let us use it for the party. Since there was so much space, my mother invited about twelve of my friends over. After eating a wonderful cream cake ordered from a French bakery, I opened my presents. Thank goodness they were all toys and games and not clothes! Then we played games—the usual pin the tail on the donkey and, because there was so much room, musical chairs. It was one of my best parties.

———— * ————

That summer my father wanted me to learn Russian, so he decided to send me to Russian school. I objected. English was my language, and I didn't want to speak any other. Besides, I understood enough Russian to know what was going on. Raising his hand as if to strike me, he yelled, "You're going and that's final!"

The next morning, after breakfast, I walked the few blocks down Seymour Road to the Russian school. I was not happy being forced to do something I was set against. Many of my Russian friends with whom I played at the Garden Apartments and at the Jewish School were there. Our teacher explained, in Russian, that no other language was to be spoken at the school. We were all to use only Russian. This made me furious. How was I to learn to speak Russian if I wasn't taught? I kept quiet during class, but when we went outside for recess, I started talking in English to my friends. No one would answer me. It was as if I didn't exist.

"Speak to me, Judy," I pleaded. "What's wrong with you?"

"We're only allowed to use Russian, Gigi. You heard the teacher." Judy answered me in Russian and ran off.

I kept persisting with my other friends— Mischa, Ize, Sophie—but it was hopeless. If I didn't speak Russian to them, they totally ignored me. It was more than I could bear. I felt like an outcast, betrayed by my own friends. I ran from the school yard, screaming like a wounded animal, and kept running until I got home.

"I won't go back there. I won't! I won't! I won't!"
I sobbed.

And that was the end of my learning to speak
Russian.

———— * ————

"Eding, please come home now; Joey just died."

Eding and I immediately stopped our game of
hopscotch in the courtyard. Shocked by the news,
I listened to Eding's father calmly ask me, "Gigi,
you'll come to our place tomorrow morning to
say good-bye to Joey?" I said I would and watched
Eding and her father walk slowly hand in hand toward their apartment.

How could Joey be dead? Just a few days ago we
were all playing games together. Joey complained
of a headache, went home, and now he was dead.
He wasn't even six years old. I ran home immediately and told my mother what had happened.

"Gigi, that's terrible," she said, hugging me.

"Eding's father wants me to see Joey before they
bury him."

"Absolutely not!" she said, holding me by the
shoulders and looking me straight in the eye.

"Why not, Mummy? He wants me to say good-
bye to Joey." I had never seen a dead person before
and wanted to look at Joey.

"What did Joey die of?" my mother asked.

"Eding's father said meningitis."

"You see, Gigi, meningitis is very contagious. Don't you remember, when your friend Mischa got it last year, how afraid the doctor was that the rest of his family would come down with it?"

"But Mischa got well, Mummy, and Joey didn't."

"I'm afraid, Gigi, you could get sick just from looking at Joey."

"But I said I'd go, Mummy. I told Eding's father I'd be by." I was pleading and didn't know what else to say.

"No, Gigi, and that's final. Your father would say the same thing."

I felt miserable that night. I didn't want to disobey my parents. I knew if I went and they found out about it, there'd be hell to pay. But I didn't want to disappoint Eding's father, and I wanted to see Joey one last time.

The next morning, after breakfast, I decided I'd have to do what I wanted. My parents were already at work. The hot August air blasted me in the face as I came out of our building. Don't dead people spoil in the heat? I wondered. Do they start to smell? I walked over to Joey's building, to the right of the main courtyard. I looked all around before entering, making sure no one saw me. Climbing the four flights of stairs, I felt a mixture of fear, sadness, and curiosity.

Joey's mother answered my knock on the door. She seemed very pleased that I came, as did Eding and Joey's father. Eding's father took me over to Joey's crib. Peering down into it, I saw Joey dressed in brown slacks, shoes, and a jacket. His hands were at his sides, and a large brown wooden cross lay on his chest. His eyes were closed, and he was absolutely still. I expected him to move at any moment, open his eyes, and announce to everyone that he was just fine. But nothing like that happened. Moving away from the crib, I suddenly felt the need to leave the apartment. I told Joey's family how sorry I was and went out the door. I stayed outside the door for a few seconds, not moving.

My heart was pounding, and then sadness filled my whole body. Tears started rolling down my cheeks, and I began sobbing. I couldn't breathe properly. I had to get away and began running down the stairs, unable to see clearly because of the tears. Why did Joey have to die? What does it mean to be dead? I kept running as fast as I could. Joey, where are you? As the outside loomed closer and I could see the sun through the doorway, I prayed to God that that silly rhyme we kids sang in fun was true. It had to be true. Please, God, let it be true!

One, two, three, four, five, six, seven.
All good children go to heaven.
When they die, they reach the sky.
One, two, three, four, five, six, seven.

CHAPTER SEVEN
A British Schoolboy

———————————

GIGI, DEAR, we're starting you in the British school this year," my mother announced one day in late August. I couldn't have been happier. I longed to attend the British school, and my wish was coming true.

"It's a beautiful school, Gigi," she said, "with lots of lawn for you to play on, and you'll be able to take the pedicab there all by yourself."

She didn't need to convince me. Didn't she know I looked upon myself as British? Besides, I jumped at the chance to be on my own in Shanghai. After all, I was seven years old and could take care of myself.

Every boy at the British school wore the same uniform, and my mother took me shopping at Wing On's for it—a navy blazer and cap, gray flannel shorts and pants, knee-high white socks, a long-sleeved white shirt, and a dark-colored necktie. I was excited. Dressing up for school seemed so official!

So, enrolled in the Shanghai British School in September 1946, I was eager to begin classes. It took almost half an hour to get to school, out in the western suburbs of Shanghai. To save time each morning, my mother and I arranged with a pedicab driver to pick me up in the courtyard of the Cosmopolitan Apartments. As I got closer to the school, I left the chaos of the city behind me. The streets were less crowded, and it was much quieter. The feeling of calmness was wonderful. The large gray school building was in a country setting, with lots of trees and huge open spaces as part of the grounds.

Since we had lunch breaks of two hours, I came home to eat Granny's delicious hot food and then returned to study for the afternoon. I was like a grown-up now, away from home mornings and afternoons. The freedom felt wonderful.

I made many new friends at school. Most of them were British, but some were German or Russian. Uta, a German girl with short red hair and freckles, had a trick false front tooth. She could slide it with her tongue so that it moved up and down between the teeth on either side, exposing a gap. I was fascinated and delighted by this stunt and asked her to "do the thing with your tooth, Uta" as often as I dared.

During gym class I learned cricket, field hockey, and something we kids called exercises. Our instructor, Mr. Portman, gave them the fancier name, calisthenics. The exercises weren't much fun, but they were a required part of the class, so we had to do them. "Raise your arms higher, Master Gregory," he'd shout as we marched along; "that's a good fellow." All teachers addressed students as Master or Miss followed by their first names. There was no Gigi here.

I soon grew to love the British school, though, not for anything academic, but because it was a part of my life that was all mine. I didn't have to share with Bobby, and I didn't have to explain myself to my parents. I felt as though I belonged there.

I also loved the openness of the vast, grassy lawn and athletic fields we used for running and playing. But the best place of all was an area in a far corner of the field we called the Jungle. It was totally wild and ungroomed. The grass and weeds were so tall you couldn't see anything beyond your nose once you were in the thick of it. There were a few mud puddles covered over by the grass, and we had to be careful to avoid stepping in them.

At every recess a few of us made a beeline for the Jungle and played our own version of hide-and-go-seek in the overgrowth. Then, in the few minutes of recess time, we'd try finding each other by following the sounds of rustling grass. Sometimes I could fool the others by standing completely still, barely breathing. When an unsuspecting friend wandered right up to me, I shouted, "Got you, Cecil!" as I grabbed his shirt sleeve. Once you were caught, you had to leave the Jungle. The person who did the capturing had to steal away as quickly as possible, because the sound of his voice had then given away his position. The one who caught the most people was the winner.

One day Cecil and Larry both stepped into a mud puddle, and the stench that came up was horrible—much worse than rotten eggs. "My God, we're in for it now," Cecil said, as he eyed his stinking, muddy legs with horror. We all knew what he meant and hoped we didn't have to be punished, too. Our teacher, Mrs. Walker, was appalled at the sight and smell of Cecil and Larry. She wouldn't let them in the classroom because they stank so. "You'll both have to see the principal for this!" she snapped and marched them up to his office.

All of us left in the room muttered among ourselves, hoping that what we thought was going to happen wouldn't. Being sent to the principal could mean only one thing: you were in for a caning. All of us feared the prospect of being caned more than anything else at school. But it was a part of the British system of discipline.

From what we heard, you had to bend down, grasp your knees, and do your best not to cry while the principal struck you on the buttocks with a wooden rod. The number of strokes given by the principal was determined by the severity of the "crime." Canings didn't happen very often, but when they did, word spread through school like wildfire.

After an eternity, Mrs. Walker returned and announced that there would be no caning this time. But because the boys were in such a "frightful mess," as Mrs. Walker put it, they were to be sent home. After that, all of us who played in the Jungle were very careful to avoid those smelly and dangerous mud puddles.

———— * ————

As Hanukkah approached one more, I heard a new kind of music at the British school—Christmas carols. They were beautiful songs, and I wanted to sing them. I tried out for the choir and was very excited to be picked to sing in the Christmas pageant. I knew about Christmas, but because our family was Jewish, we didn't celebrate it. I saw nothing wrong with singing beautiful songs at Christmastime, but Granny and my mother felt differently.

"I think Christmas carols are beautiful, too, Gigi," my mother said. "But they're about Jesus, and we don't pray to Jesus."

"They're not all about Jesus, Mummy," I said. "Besides, I won't be praying to Him; I'll be singing songs."

My mother took me outside our apartment so that we could speak privately. As we sat on the steps, she said, "Gigi, dear, I've never told you this before, but when I lived in Hong Kong, I went to an Italian Catholic school until I was nine years old. Granny wasn't happy about it. Can you imagine how she felt? The daughter of a Jewish rabbi going to a Christian school? But my Uncle Elias, who was supporting us then, thought it was the best school, so he enrolled me there anyway. I learned Christmas carols and even won religious medals. I was proud of them, but when I showed them to Granny, she was furious."

"So it's Granny who doesn't want me to sing Christmas carols?" I asked.

"Yes, Gigi. But I think we can work something out." The look of an idea lit up in my mother's eyes.

We went back inside, and Mother and Granny had a heated discussion in Arabic for a few minutes. I didn't know what to make of it. Then Mother said, "Granny says it's all right to sing Christmas carols if you don't sing Jesus's name or call him the lord. Will you do that for her, Gigi?"

This was very strange, I thought. But since it meant I could be in the choir, I didn't question it; I just agreed. During rehearsals I sang all the words. And when we sang "Adeste Fidelis" in Latin, I sang all the words. But I will always remember the chorus of the English version of "Oh Come, All Ye Faithful," as it soared to its musical climax during the performance for our parents and family as

Oh come, let us adore Him,
Oh come, let us adore Him,
Oh come, let us adore Hi-im,
Hm-mm, hum hum.

———— * ————

In the spring of 1947, things were going well for me at the British school, where I was about to complete my first year. I felt completely at home there, where I was perfecting my British accent and learning all about the British Empire and how great it was.

Getting to and from school each day on my own was something I looked forward to. Sometimes, though, the traffic came to a complete standstill for a few minutes, with cars, trucks, buses, bicycles, pedicabs, rickshaws, and large wheelbarrows pulled by coolies all competing for a limited amount of space. The constant beeping and tooting of horns didn't help speed things up, but the drivers kept at it anyway.

Closer to the school there were large estates, each surrounded by high walls to keep busybodies out. Some of the walls had sharp pieces of glass embedded on top to discourage intruders. Paul, a British schoolmate of mine, lived in one of those mansions; once he invited me to spend a day there with him and his family. They even had their own chauffeur come to pick me up at home! Paul's family also had a staff, consisting of a cook, gardener, and several amahs. His home was lovely, but I wouldn't have known what to do with so much space.

One afternoon at school I did a stupid thing. During English class, Vera quietly asked me to pass a note along to Larry, who sat next to me. I took the note from her. To be cute, and also to annoy Vera, I began reading it myself. Vera became agitated, and Mrs. Walker noticed. "Master Gregory, the only material you ought to be reading is the text in front of you. Since you are obviously reading something else, would you be so kind as to share it with the rest of the class?" I froze. What should I do? I looked over at Vera, who stared back at me in horror. To refuse meant I'd have to go to the principal's office.

"Well, Master Gregory, we're all waiting," Mrs. Walker said, her voice cutting the air like ice. I gulped and said, "My dear Larry, do you feel the same way about me as I do about you? Love and kisses, V."

The students roared with laughter. Mrs. Walker banged on her desk and stood up, trying to restore order in the room. Vera was in tears, and Larry leaned over and said to me, "I'm taking care of you after school." Good God, what a mess I had made of things! I couldn't concentrate for the rest of the day. Larry was big and strong and had a reputation for knowing how to take care of himself. And I was terrified of being beaten up. I'd seen movies where Humphrey Bogart or Gary Cooper got into fights, and it didn't look like any fun. What would my parents say if I showed up at home with a black eye?

The dismissal bell rang at four o'clock, and Larry and a few of his friends were waiting for me near the pedicab stand when I came outside. Are they all going to beat me up? I wondered. Larry motioned me to follow him to the side of the building, away from people and traffic. Suddenly, he grabbed me by my shirt collar, and I heard my books falling to the ground. He pulled me right up against him and said through gritted teeth, "I'm going to punch your face."

"Look, Larry," I pleaded, "I'm truly sorry about the note. I meant no harm. It was stupid of me. Please don't hit me!"

He pushed me away roughly; then he grabbed me by my arm and squeezed it tightly. "Don't you ever embarrass me like that again," he yelled. Then he punched my arm hard and let me go. "You little sissy," he said with disgust, and stomped off with his friends.

I felt just awful, but very lucky. Why didn't he beat me up? Why did I do such a dumb thing? I liked Larry and Vera. How could I hurt them like that? After this incident, things were never the same between Larry and me. He stopped playing with me, and we hardly ever spoke.

———— * ————

In late spring, Baba was taken ill and hospital-ized for a gallbladder condition. "Is it very serious, Daddy? Will Baba be all right?"

My father explained that Baba had gallstones and that the only cure was to remove the gallbladder. "They're operating on her tomorrow," he said. "She should be fine." My father spent most of the night after Baba's surgery at the hospital. Appar-ently, there had been complications. When I awoke the next morning, he was standing up, smoking his pipe and looking out the window.

"How's Baba, Daddy?" I asked.

His answer came quietly. "Baba died last night, Gigi." He sounded so sad. I buried my head in the pillow and cried. My father consoled me, hugging me to make me feel better. The times I could always count on him to be kind and loving to me, like he was now, were when I was ill. I cherished these at-tentions. I wasn't ill this morning, but this was not an ordinary situation. My parents said I could stay home from school that day. A death in the family was a good enough excuse to be absent.

I moped at home all day. I didn't even feel like going outside. Everyone was upset, especially my father. Aunt Luba and Uncle Boris came over to comfort him and to be comforted by him and my mother. They also discussed funeral arrangements for Baba. After Luba and Boris left, I asked my parents if I could go to Baba's funeral. "No," I was told. "Funerals are no place for children. They are too sad." No matter what I said, my parents would not change their minds. I was very disappointed. Not going to Baba's funeral deprived me of saying a last good-bye to her.

——— * ———

Soon it was summer, with the weather hot and humid, as usual. I desperately wanted a bicycle and begged my parents to buy me one. "No, Gigi," came the reply, "that's out of the question. It's too dangerous."

"But I promise to ride it only in the courtyard. Teddy has a bike."

"Gigi, it is just not safe in the courtyard with so many cars coming in and out all the time. Don't you remember only last week that beautiful German shepherd dog was killed?"

It was simply no use arguing with them. All my parents could do was go on about the dangers, naming people they knew personally who had been run over while riding bicycles. And they reminded me that not long ago even one of my schoolmates had her head crushed under the wheels of a truck.

Instead, they bought me a pair of roller skates. They felt skates were a lot safer than a bicycle. Teddy and Dolly also had skates, so we skated together in the courtyard often. I still wanted a bike, and Teddy let me ride hers secretly once in a while when my parents were away from home. But it was wonderful zooming through the Cosmopolitan Apartment alleyways on skates. Sometimes we even had races there. I spent practically every evening on my skates. It was much more comfortable playing out of doors during the heat of summer than being cooped up in our hot and stuffy apartment.

Toward the end of the summer, my parents were worried because I had become too thin. They took me to Dr. Glass, our family physician, who was concerned that I might come down with tuberculosis. We called it TB. Victims of the disease were all over Shanghai—thin, wasted bodies, hacking and coughing up blood in the streets. It never dawned on me I might become like that, and I refused to believe such a thing could happen to me.

Loss of weight was a bad sign, and too much exercising was not healthy, Dr. Glass said. At least that's what he believed at the time. The prescription: no more roller-skating until I gained more weight. I was furious. Who was he to tell me what to do? "What if I only skated a little bit each day?" I pleaded. "I promise not to go very fast." But Dr. Glass said absolutely not, and my parents went along with him.

My skates were taken from me and given away. The doctor had even told me I was not to play very hard. "Don't exert yourself, Gigi," he ordered me, "it's not good for the lungs." I felt frustrated and angry. Didn't my parents know how much skating meant to me? Oh, how I wished I was back at school. I could play in the Jungle, and Dr. Glass and my parents would never know. To make matters worse, I was given Klim to drink—an awful-tasting powdered milk that you mixed with water. It was supposed to build up my strength, but it made me want to throw up instead.

What was I to do for fun? I went to the movies more and more—*Gone with the Wind,* Walt Disney's *Bambi* and *Fantasia,* John Wayne films, and countless others. Movies comforted me in a way nothing else could, and I felt protected in the darkened theatre.

It turned out that this was to be my last year on Seymour road. In the spring of 1948, by a stroke of luck, my parents, Bobby, and I would be living in a large apartment nearby with my Uncle Boris and Aunt Luba.

CHAPTER EIGHT

A New Home

* —————————————————————— *

THE FREEDMAN APARTMENTS, our new home
on Ferry Road, was a palace compared to
Granny's room. It even had a telephone and hot
running water. Aunt Luba's boss had turned the
apartment over to her when he decided to leave
Shanghai with his family. Because he asked for
none of the usual key money—normally several
thousand dollars just for the privilege of renting a
place—Luba and Boris could afford the rent. But
the apartment was too large for them, so they asked
us if we'd like to share it. My parents jumped at
the chance. At last Granny could have her place to
herself. Living together in one room for over six
years had not been easy for anyone.

Our apartment was on the fifth floor of a six-
story dark gray building. Because the building was
on a corner and was the tallest structure in the
neighborhood, the rooms were always bright. We
had two balconies that faced Bubbling Well Road,

about two blocks away, which I could see clearly. I spent a lot of time out on the balconies enjoying the view from high up and watching people in the bustling street below going about their business. Despite the relative wealth of the apartments' tenants, we were surrounded by poverty. Beggars were always in the streets. Poor old Chinese men and women lived in small shacks across the road from us.

My parents, Bobby, and I still shared a bedroom, but it was about three times larger than Granny's apartment. To my delight, the building even had an elevator.

A beautifully kept courtyard ran between our building and the second building of the apartment complex behind us. The courtyard was much smaller than the one at Seymour Road, too small to skate in. But it didn't matter, since I wasn't allowed to roller-skate anymore. We were only about a five-minute walk from Granny, so we visited her often, and I saw and played with Dolly occasionally.

Since my parents were doing well financially, we had our own cook and an amah. Luba and Boris also had a cook. The two cooks prepared completely different meals—one for Luba and Boris and one for us. What a treat it was to be served and waited on in a real dining room. But I was fascinated with what the cooks fixed for themselves, convinced that what they ate was far tastier than the food they cooked for us. It certainly smelled better. Often I'd go into the kitchen after dinner to see if they'd let me taste some of their food. It was always delicious, and I wanted to eat it instead of ours. A dish with sour cabbage became a favorite of mine. I loved Chinese food, but our cook never fixed it for us because my father didn't care for it.

One night my mother caught me in the kitchen and pulled me out of there as if I'd committed a crime. "Gigi," she said in a scolding tone, "don't go begging from the cooks. They buy their own food and cook it here, and they can't afford to feed you."

"Mummy, I'm really sorry. I didn't know."

"We don't pay them very much, Gigi, only about what it costs to buy a sack of rice each month. So don't bother them."

I felt ashamed, and I obeyed my mother. But I still wanted to eat their food anyway. Boris and Luba's cook, a Chinese woman named Doonya, also spoke Russian, which pleased them very much. She knew how to cook Russian food, and that's what she always prepared for them. Sometimes Doonya cooked for all of us, and I liked most of what she made. But once she served fried brains. They were soft and mushy, and I could barely force myself to eat. After that experience, I wasn't so sure about Doonya's cooking anymore.

There was also an upright piano in our apartment, and I was eager to begin taking lessons. My cousin Becky, a few years older than I, was an excellent pianist, and I wished I could play like her. At the British school I heard an older student, Helen

Papanoff, practice the piano, and I'd hang around listening to her when I should've been somewhere else. Then I saw the movie *Anchors Aweigh*. In it there's a remarkable scene with about fifty pianists playing the same song on fifty grand pianos in the Hollywood Bowl. What a spectacle! That settled it. I was going to master the piano.

My teacher, a sweet Russian lady, came to our apartment at seven o'clock in the evening once a week and gave me a one-hour lesson. I always looked forward to these sessions, and I practiced every afternoon when I came home from school. I even enjoyed the five-finger exercises. Chopin became my favorite composer, but his music was too difficult for me to play. I did get to hear it, though, on the radio and in the film about his life, *A Song to Remember*.

We had a large shortwave radio set in the living room, and we occasionally received broadcasts from the United States. One program I heard, hosted by the comedian Red Skelton, was about something he called Kid's Day, a special day set aside just for children to have fun and play games. I wished I could go to America and take part in that day.

About this time I saw the movie musical *State Fair*. I was amazed by some of the scenes at the fair—Ferris wheels; merry-go-rounds; pig-judging contests; and most of all, something called cotton candy. In the movie it was pink, and a girl about my age who had freckles ate the delicious-looking fluff. We had none of those things in Shanghai. Everything looked like so much fun I wanted to experience it myself.

We also had a phonograph and many records of American and Russian songs. I loved Russian music, and so did Bobby. He learned to recognize some records by their labels. When he wanted to listen to one of them, he pulled it out of the rack and asked one of us to play it for him. He spoke well enough for me to understand him by then, and we got along very well.

Bobby couldn't say *s* words properly yet. He'd say *f* instead. Uncle Jason used to laugh hilariously when Bobby substituted *f* for *s* in certain words. Bobby didn't understand what was going on, but he'd join in and laugh right along with us anyway.

At about this time, my parents and Luba and Boris decided to apply for visas to come to America. Trouble was brewing again in Shanghai. The Communists, led by Mao Zedong, were gaining strength in China. Chiang Kai-shek, the leader of China's ruling Nationalist party and an ally of the United States, was losing ground. Living under a Communist regime was something my family wanted to avoid. They were afraid of losing personal freedom as well as the newfound prosperity they had earned since the end of World War II.

My father told me that America was the land of opportunity and freedom, and that's why he wanted us to move there. His family had fled Russia soon after the Russian Communists took over, and he wanted to avoid Communist rule in China, too. He also told me that Baba had visited America a couple of times as a young girl, and stories of her visits had always fascinated him and Aunt Luba. This was the first I had heard of this! Someone in my family had actually been to America. Not only that, my father told me we had distant cousins living there.

These relatives of our family, living in Buffalo, New York, agreed to sponsor our coming to America. It was a huge responsibility. They had to promise the U.S. government that they'd be personally responsible for our welfare for up to five years, if necessary. My father, Luba, and Boris all applied under the Russian quota. With the quota system, only a certain number of people with a particular nationality were admitted into the United States each year. Some countries were given small quotas; others had larger ones. In 1948, relations between Russia and the United States were friendly, and the Russian quota was fairly large. Of course, the Communist rulers in Russia didn't allow citizens of that country to apply to leave, but Russian citizens living outside of Russia, like my father, weren't under such restrictions. My mother, Bobby, and I were included under the same quota, since we would be traveling with my father. My British citizenship was of no importance. Once the applications were made, it was a matter of time until the U.S. government acted on them.

———— * ————

I celebrated my ninth birthday in May of 1948. As a special treat, Uncle Boris took me shopping for one of the nicest presents I ever received: a pair of pigeons. I had always wanted a pet, but that was out of the question on Seymour Road. Aunt Luba had a cute Pekingese dog named Mimi, which Bobby and I loved. But now I was going to have pets of my very own.

I named them Betsy and John, after a young girl and boy who loved each other in an Elizabeth Taylor movie. The pigeons were gray, with black stripes near the edges of their wings. I kept them in a cage on the living room balcony. They soon came to recognize me and act excited when they saw me. Whenever I approached, they'd both stamp their bright red feet up and down quickly and flutter about the cage. Each afternoon I let them out for their daily exercise. Betsy flew away for a few minutes and then returned to John. He couldn't fly because one of his wings had been clipped. That way Betsy always returned. Because Betsy and John were a mated pair, one would never desert the other unless one of them died. It was very romantic.

Uncle Boris loved animals, especially birds. He had his own pet chicken at the Metropole Hotel downtown, where he worked in the stock room.

The bird followed him all over the place, and he spoke to it in Russian as if it were a person.

———— * ————

In September of 1948, Dolly left Shanghai with her parents for the newly founded state of Israel. When I found out she was leaving, I was crushed. I wanted to say a proper good-bye to her and see her off at the ship. My father and I arrived at the dock after everyone had boarded, so I ran up and down alongside the ship to see if I could spot her on deck.

I saw her father, Grisha, at the ship's stern, waving to some people, but there was no Dolly or her mother, Fanny.

"Uncle Grisha," I yelled, "where's Dolly?" But he didn't hear or see me. Just then the band started playing the stirring Jewish national anthem, "Hatikva," and it was impossible to hear a voice above the music. I waved my arms wildly, trying to get his attention, but it was no use.

I hurried back to my father anxiously and told him I couldn't find Dolly. He put his arm around my shoulder, and I leaned against him. The ship started pulling away from the dock, taking Dolly with it. The music got louder and louder. I always cried anyway when I heard "Hatikva," but this time it was much worse. As the tears rolled down my cheeks, I wondered if I'd ever see Dolly again. I'll miss you, Dolly, I said to myself silently. I waved feebly one last time, and then we went home.

———— * ————

I felt as if my life had been thrown off balance. Even Jewish holidays weren't the same once we stopped living with Granny. It was Granny who kept the traditions, and when we were no longer with her, things were different. My father and Aunt Luba were never very religious, and Uncle Boris wasn't even Jewish. My mother tried the best she could to maintain a Jewish home, but it was a lost cause. We no longer observed the Sabbath, pork was allowed in the kitchen, and we resorted to using a menorah at Hanukkah instead of the more traditional oil lamps.

We still went to Uncle Shaul's house for Passover seders, and we ate matzo instead of bread during Passover. We also went to synagogue for the High Holy Days. But the feeling behind these observances just wasn't the same without Granny. We were going through the motions instead of living the religion as Granny did.

CHAPTER NINE

Upheaval

* —————————————————— *

I WAS WELL INTO my second year at the British school. The school became more and more important to me. I had an identity there that was real, and I lived it each day. I sang "God Save the King" and "Rule Britannia" with all my heart. Being British and being accepted as a Britisher were like a substitute religion.

Then, early one morning in April 1949, my sleep was shattered by the rat-a-tat-tat of machine guns in the street. I sprang up in my bed and saw my father crawling on his belly toward the balcony. My mother, still half asleep, yelled at him to come back. Frantically, she ran to get Uncle Boris. "*Doorak! Doorak!* Joe," Boris screamed, calling my father a stupid fool, and dragging him by his ankles back into the room. "Do you want to get killed?"

All of us were scared and confused. Only yesterday we had watched a joyful parade of Nationalist Army forces and their civilian supporters from our bedroom balcony. People were dressed in costumes, and there was a huge figure of Chiang Kai-shek to show what a strong leader he was. The mood was festive and happy. The parade made its way noisily down Ferry Road, and I kept track of the throng of merrymakers as they made their way to Bubbling Well Road and onward toward downtown.

And now yesterday's celebration was replaced by the heart-stopping sounds of bullets. What was going on? We stayed far away from the windows and balconies until we heard no more gunfire. Soon loud voices yelling in Chinese drifted up into our rooms. Cautiously my father and Boris peered outside and motioned us to have a look for ourselves. I couldn't believe what I saw. Sandbags were piled on top of one another at the street corners. Dozens of Chiang Kai-shek's soldiers, some of them limping from their wounds, were being marched away at gunpoint by Mao Zedong's forces. The thing my family feared most had happened: Shanghai was now under Communist control.

For months there had been reports that Chiang Kai-shek was going to be overthrown by the Communists, but most people didn't want to believe it. Mao kept building up strength. His armies had already captured the major cities of Peking and Nanking a few weeks earlier. The attack on Shanghai by Mao's forces had taken the Nationalist Army by complete surprise. Overnight, China was his.

Mao took control immediately. All businesses were to operate normally, including those owned by foreigners, and life would continue as usual. The move was to prevent the population from falling into a general panic. The adults in the family continued in their same jobs, while I kept going to the British school. Within a couple of weeks, things seemed no different to me than before the Communists came.

———— * ————

One evening about two months later, my mother and father were very late coming home from work. I didn't know what was keeping them and became very worried. Luba and Boris were as confused as I. When my parents finally arrived, Mother was a wreck. I'd never seen her so upset, and it frightened me. She told us her Chinese co-workers, people she thought of as friends, had held her hostage for the whole day. They had demanded to be paid more money. When she explained there was no extra money, they decided to hold her for ransom.

Somehow my mother had managed to call my father, and he brought a policeman to her office. The officer ordered the employees to release her. As she was leaving, the workers threatened to come to our apartment and demand to be fed and cared for if she didn't pay them the money they wanted. This is what had scared her so much. She felt powerless if the employees were to carry out their threat.

After that incident, Mother didn't go back to work again. Her company was about to close its office anyway because it had nothing to sell and because no more cargo ships were coming to Shanghai. Once again, my father was bringing in the only money to support us. The workers never came to our home, but my mother lived in fear for months.

My family began to worry if we'd ever be able to leave Shanghai. The American Consulate couldn't give us any information on our visas, and we didn't know how much longer the Chinese would let foreigners depart. We certainly didn't want to be trapped in Communist China.

———— * ————

In September my parents, Bobby, and I moved into our own apartment in downtown Shanghai. My father was doing quite well in his job as office manager. Since his company sold imported goods—refrigerators, freezers, radios—and no more were coming into Shanghai, those still remaining in the warehouse brought premium prices.

By this time most foreigners were getting out of China, and my father managed to take over an apartment from some Americans who had returned to the United States. My parents didn't own much furniture, so my mother borrowed some that had been stored by her former boss. There was even a piano, so I happily continued with my weekly lessons. My parents were delighted to finally have a home all to themselves. After all these years, they didn't have to share with anyone. Still, we all slept in the same large bedroom. The other bedroom was for our live-in cook.

Our new home was the most wonderful place —a penthouse on the ninth floor of Hamilton House, right across the street from the Metropole Hotel, where Uncle Boris worked, and only a block or so away from the Bund. The rooms were large and bright. The best things about the apartment were the two huge red-tiled terraces. One was so large you could play tennis on it. The view from there was sensational.

I spent many happy afternoons on the terraces with my pigeons. John had plenty of space to wander around, since he couldn't fly. One afternoon I couldn't find him. I looked everywhere, with the help of our cook and our amah, but he was nowhere to be found. I was heartbroken. What could have happened? There was an air shaft that came up through the largest terrace. The only thing we could guess was that John somehow slipped into the shaft and fell nine stories to his death. Poor John. I felt so sorry for him. Betsy was very upset. When I let her out for her daily exercises, she fluttered around and around, looking for John. One day she flew away and didn't return. I cried and prayed she'd come back, but she never did. Since John was gone, there was nothing to keep Betsy with me.

When Uncle Boris heard of the tragedy, he bought me a new pair of pigeons right away. They were both pure white. I didn't have the heart to give them real names, so I called them Whitey Boy and Whitey Girl. They were beautiful birds. But even though I enjoyed having them, they never could replace John and Betsy.

———— * ————

Soon the bombing started again. For four years we had enjoyed peace in Shanghai, and now we were being attacked once more. This time, though, it wasn't the Japanese, but Chiang Kai-shek's pilots. Chiang was not about to give up China, so he started bombing major cities in an effort to scare the Communists away. Most of the bombs fell on Pootung, across from the Bund, and in outlying areas. But a bomb could always fall in a heavily populated zone by mistake. Bobby became terrified of the air-raid sirens, the low-flying airplanes, and the sound of antiaircraft fire. Whenever planes flew overhead, he ran away and hid, screaming "Air raid, air raid." Sometimes I'd hide with him. He was just about the age I was when I went through the same thing in World War II, so I knew how scared he must be. Comforting my brother made me feel good.

One afternoon at the British school, the air-raid siren sounded just as we were about to be dismissed for the day. All the students and teachers gathered together in the auditorium for safety. No one knew what was happening, and everyone seemed confused. Then I heard someone yell out, "The Palace Hotel's been bombed!"

I panicked. "But my father works right across the street from there!" I screamed, afraid something terrible had happened to him. I started crying.

"Slap him; he's hysterical," shouted Vera.

"I am not hysterical!" I yelled back at her between sobs. I was convinced Vera wanted to get back at me for the note incident. One of the teachers took me aside and calmed me down. Soon the all clear sounded, and we were allowed to leave. I tried calling home, but the telephone lines were dead.

I grabbed the first pedicab to come by and started home, afraid of what I'd learn when I arrived. Was my father all right? If he was hurt, was he badly injured? What if he had been killed? The trip home seemed to take forever, and all along the way I was in my own world, worrying about my father. I kept looking for signs of smoke as we got closer to downtown. Finally the pedicab driver dropped me off outside our building. I was home. As soon as I got off the elevator, I ran to our door. Rushing into the apartment, I yelled, "Is Daddy all right, Mummy?"

She was puzzled. "Why, yes, dear. I suppose so." Thank God! The bombing of the Palace Hotel had been only a rumor. My mother assured me that the hotel had not been bombed. Bombs had fallen in Pootung, across the river. But no bombs were dropped anywhere near the Bund. My father was safe. I had never felt so relieved in my life.

—————— * ——————

By the winter of 1949, people became desperate to leave Shanghai. The Communist government had announced it would take over all foreign businesses, and no foreigners wanted to continue living under Communist rule. The value of Chinese money was falling daily. Twice a month my father brought home his pay—two large boxes filled with money. It was almost comical. All that money, and it was hardly worth the paper it was printed on. The currency was called *Jhen Ming Piao* in Chinese, but we renamed it Just More Paper.

My parents were becoming very concerned about getting visas for the United States. The American Consulate in Shanghai was about to close, and if that happened, there would be no way for us to leave for America. To be safe, my parents also applied for visas to Israel. Those were issued without trouble if one was Jewish. Maybe I'd see Dolly again after all! Uncle Jason and his family had also decided to move to Israel, and Granny would travel with them. Many of our non-Jewish friends obtained visas to any country that would have them, sometimes paying huge sums of money.

I prayed we'd get to go to America for purely selfish reasons. Maybe I'd get to see George again. I'd learned so many exciting things about America from all those wonderful movies I had seen and from listening to shortwave radio broadcasts. I wanted to see for myself if they were true. My biggest wish was that we'd live in Hollywood so that I could be in the movies myself. Nothing could be better than that. I hadn't even thought of the difficulties my parents would be facing beginning life all over again in a new country.

In January 1950, my mother received a telephone call saying that our visas had arrived. She was ecstatic. Her happiness, however, lasted only a few minutes because the call turned out to be a prank. One of her cousins, knowing how concerned my parents were about going to America, played this cruel joke. My mother never forgave her. Two weeks later she received another call saying our visas to America had come. At first she didn't believe it, but this time it was true. My father went to pick them up personally. Not only had our visas come, but those of Boris and Luba had come as well. We had just made it—our family had gotten six of the last ten visas from Shanghai to the United States. After that, the American Consulate closed its doors for good.

Once we had our visas in hand, my parents applied for exit visas. The exit visa allowed one to leave China. Without it you were trapped. It didn't matter if you had a visa to a foreign country. So now the waiting began all over again. In the meantime, we all had to take physical exams before being allowed to enter the United States. If any of us had a serious illness, such as TB, we wouldn't be admitted to America. Luckily, all of us passed the exam. Dr. Glass and my parents needn't have worried about my health after all, for I never came down with tuberculosis.

———— * ————

Soon after receiving our visas to go to America, we moved back in with Boris and Luba on Ferry Road. Aunt Luba had suggested it as a way for my parents to save money. The Hamilton House apartment had been very expensive, and we needed money for the trip to the United States. My parents were never good at saving money, and now things were tight again. My mother returned all our borrowed furniture to the warehouse, and we were once again living closer to Granny. But I missed the Hamilton House apartment very much. I had loved the large rooms, spacious terraces, and being so close to the Bund. I brought Whitey Girl and Whitey Boy with me to Ferry Road, but I didn't keep them long. We could receive our exit visas at any moment, and I wanted to find a good home for them. Watson Feng, my father's boss, suggested his nephew Tak Sun might want them. I was sorry to see them go, but I knew they'd be in good hands.

At this time I also withdrew from the British school and stopped taking piano lessons. These were also steps my parents had to take to save money. I still practiced the piano on my own. But I missed school and all my friends there very much. My British identity was tied to the school, and I felt lost and at sea without it. I was very confused. On the one hand, I wanted to go to America so that I could be in the movies. But I also wanted to be British at the same time. I was in a terrible state, and there was no one I could talk to about it.

My parents and Luba and Boris began packing. Exit visas were announced in the newspaper daily. Every morning I anxiously ran down to the news-stand on the corner and hurried back home with a paper. My father tore open the pages to the proper spot and ran his finger down the column of names. "Nothing again, dammit" was his usual disgusted response.

One day my father's name was listed, but the rest of us weren't. He was furious. Exit visas were valid only for a limited amount of time. If you didn't leave before the date stamped on the visa, you might never be able to get out. The only ships leaving China before my father's exit visa expired were from the port city of Tientsin, a few hundred miles to the north. My father booked passage for my mother, Bobby, and me on the Dutch freighter *Heinrick Jessen*. He was taking a big chance. What if the rest of us didn't get our visas in time? The money spent on tickets would be wasted. The *Heinrick Jessen* would take us to Hong Kong. From there we had tickets on an American ship, the *General Gordon,* to San Francisco.

I rushed to the newspaper stand each morning for a couple of weeks to check for our names. Boris and Luba's names finally appeared. My aunt and uncle's exit visas expired later than my father's, so they arranged to travel directly from Shanghai to Hong Kong. We would join them there. My mother, Bobby, and I still needed our exit visas, and we were getting worried. If we didn't get them before my father had to leave, he would have to go by himself. No one wanted to risk asking for an extension of an exit visa.

On a cold morning in April our names finally appeared in the paper. I rushed home as fast as I could with the good news. We had only a few days before my father's exit visa expired, so there was not a moment to lose. It had been just about a year since Mao Zedong's army conquered Shanghai. My father reserved space for us on a train to Tientsin. We had to settle for ordinary nonsleeper seats, and we were lucky to get them. The train was already fully booked with people getting out of China. Practically all Westerners still in Shanghai were leaving to catch a ship from Tientsin.

On the morning we departed from Shanghai, all of us gathered in the living room of our apartment one last time and sat down for a moment of total silence. Everyone was absolutely still. This was a Russian custom that had something to do with good luck before leaving on a long journey.

My father hired several pedicabs to take us to the train station. We had huge steamer trunks, suitcases, and Oriental rugs to transport, and that was the cheapest way of doing it. At the station, porters took care of all our baggage and loaded it onto the long train. Uncle Jason brought Granny to say good-bye to us. She was dressed in a dark, heavy overcoat, since it was chilly and overcast. One by one, she and Uncle Jason hugged and kissed all of us. My mother and Granny cried and said some things to each other in Arabic. Wiping the tears from our eyes, we boarded the train quickly.

We took our seats—very uncomfortable hard wooden ones—and waited for the train to leave. I spotted Granny from a window and waved good-bye. She was still crying. Will I ever see you again, Granny? Just then the train jerked and started to pull away. I kept waving to Granny until I couldn't see her anymore, and we were on our way.

CHAPTER TEN

Journey to America

————————————

A S OUR TRAIN SPED away from Shanghai, I was struck by the beautiful Chinese countryside. I had never seen so much empty space and so few people. It was my first trip out of the city and the first time I'd ever been on a train. We made frequent stops for food, and I welcomed the rest from the constant clackety-clack of the wheels rolling over the tracks. The trip to Tientsin was long and uncomfortable, and I could not sleep with all the unfamiliar noises around me. My mother and Bobby were having an especially hard time. Fortunately, a friend of my mother's on the train had a sleeping berth, and she let Mother and Bobby use it for a few hours.

By the time we arrived in Tientsin the next morning, we were all exhausted. Our ship wasn't scheduled to leave for three days, so my father's first job was to find us a hotel. In the rush to leave Shanghai, my parents hadn't thought to make reservations ahead, and all the hotels were filled with foreigners waiting to depart China. The manager of the Canterbury Hotel, seeing the sorry state we were in, went out of his way to fix up a small room for us. We squeezed into it with all of our baggage. Bobby kept asking, "Is this our new home?" He would be repeating this question many times on our trip.

On the morning we were to leave Tientsin, we arrived late at the dock. This worried my parents because the ship's accommodations were going to be assigned on a first-come-first-served basis. There seemed to be thousands of people crammed into a very small area. My Aunt Sally, who was traveling to Australia by way of Hong Kong, had arrived hours before us. She wanted to make sure of a choice place on the ship.

At the last moment before boarding, the Chinese officials played a cruel trick on the early arrivals. They reversed their position, turning the inspection stand to face the latecomers. By pure dumb luck, we, who had been the last to arrive, were the first to be processed. The officials checked all of our documents and found everything in order. Then they searched each of us—patting all over our bodies with their flattened hands—in full view of everyone else. This caused my mother great embarrassment. I thought it was fun because it made me feel important.

The Chinese were looking for American money

because it was forbidden to leave China with any. While we were being searched, several officials began checking other passengers. One, a Catholic priest, got into real trouble. He had hidden some U.S. dollars inside the felt headband of his hat, and the Chinese found it. They took it all away, of course, and yelled at him for trying to get away with smuggling. Luckily, they did not keep him from leaving China.

When my father saw what happened to the priest, he became nervous. While we were waiting for the boarding process to begin, a friend of my father's had come up to him and quietly handed him a twenty-dollar bill. The man was repaying an old debt, but my father didn't know what to do with the money. While no one was looking, he removed a bit of cotton from the inside of his lighter, stuffed the bill inside, and covered it over with the cotton he'd removed. In those days cotton was used in lighters to soak up flammable lighter fluid. The fluid passed from the cotton to the wick. As the official's hands roamed over my father's body, Dad took out the lighter and lit his pipe with it. Time seemed to stand still as my father puffed away, waiting for the tobacco to ignite. "Finish, finish," the official said, waving my father away. He replaced the lighter in his coat pocket, and the moment of crisis was over.

The officials wouldn't allow us to take all our belongings. The Oriental rugs hadn't been cleaned properly, so we had no choice but to leave them on the dock. "I wonder which of them will get to keep the rugs?" my mother said bitterly.

We stepped on a wide wooden gangplank and made our way onto the ship. I turned back to look at the crowd and saw my poor Aunt Sally, who had been waiting for so many hours, on the verge of tears. A Danish sailor led us to a huge cargo area that had been converted into the largest bedroom in the world. Hundreds of cots covered the floor, and my parents spent several minutes deciding where we should sleep. They picked a corner for the most privacy, and we began settling in. We were not allowed to save a space for Aunt Sally; she had been assigned to a different sleeping area. Because the *Heinrick Jessen* was a freighter, and since so many people were anxious to leave China, the ship was filled to beyond capacity.

It took several hours before everyone was on

board, and I couldn't wait to find out what traveling on a big ship was like. Tientsin was on the Hai River, and we would have to travel several miles before the river emptied into the Gulf of Chihli. Uncle Jason had told me once that the most amazing thing about traveling from a river to the sea was the change in color of the water. "Gigi," he said, "the river is brown, and then all of a sudden the seawater is green. You can actually see the dividing line." By late afternoon we left Tientsin, and I was staring at the brown, muddy water of the river, waiting for it to mingle with the sea. When was it going to happen? Then it was time to eat. I didn't want to miss the color change, but I had to eat when it was our turn.

Reluctantly I left the railing and went below. Our food was served cafeteria style, which I had never experienced before. It seemed strange to have someone plop food on my plate when I was used to taking what I wanted. I ate as fast as I could and dashed back up on deck. Everywhere I looked, the water was a beautiful green color. Darn it! I had missed the magic moment. But I imagined that I had seen the line between river water and seawater. Later that night, after I had met some children about my age, I said to them, "Did you see where the river met the sea? Wasn't it the best thing you ever saw?"

———— * ————

We traveled through calm waters on our five-day voyage to Hong Kong. Despite the crowded conditions on board, I had a wonderful time. The food was tasty, and the crew was friendly and helpful. Hong Kong harbor was spectacularly beautiful. My mother pointed out Victoria Peak to me and said, "Gigi, dear, you were born way up there." My mother hadn't been to Hong Kong, her childhood home, since my birth almost eleven years before. She was anxious to see all her old friends again. We docked on the mainland side of the harbor, not Hong Kong Island itself, and went to the Kowloon Hotel. We were shown to a huge, luxurious room, which delighted all of us. How nice it was to have space and privacy again.

Hong Kong Airport was near the hotel, and poor Bobby kept running to my mother and grabbing her skirt, yelling, "Air raid, air raid," every time he heard or saw a plane. No matter what my mother said or did to try to assure him it wasn't an air raid, he kept acting this way whenever an airplane flew over. I felt so sorry for him.

Over the next five days, while waiting for the *General Gordon* to arrive, we toured Hong Kong Island and Kowloon. It was a beautiful place, and the weather was warm and sunny. Because Hong Kong is in the tropics, people there wear light clothing most of the year. We visited Repulse Bay, which had a gorgeous, sandy beach and the most remarkable water I had ever seen—crystal clear and a lovely turquoise color. I was amazed that I could see the sandy bottom to a depth of ten feet or more.

The layover in Hong Kong provided a wonderful rest for my parents. They had a great time seeing old friends, and it pleased me to see them so happy. They were finally able to relax following the tense weeks before our departure from Shanghai. The remainder of our trip was not going to be so pleasant—three and a half weeks of traveling in rough seas to Manila, Japan, and Honolulu before finally arriving in San Francisco. Our accommodations on the *General Gordon* were going to be an unpleasant surprise.

———— * ————

Boris and Luba greeted us when we boarded the new ship, and it felt good to be reunited with them. A converted Army troop carrier, the *General Gordon* was transporting close to two thousand passengers. There were two classes of accommodations: first and steerage. It was out of the question for my family to pay for first-class passage, since they'd need all their money to begin new lives in San Francisco. In steerage the men and women slept in separate parts of the ship. I stayed with my father, while Bobby was with my mother. But we spent the rest of our time together in other parts of the ship and ate in the same dining hall. As on the *Heinrick Jessen,* the food was served cafeteria style. But unlike the meals on the Danish ship, those served on the *General Gordon* were dreadful.

Mother and Bobby slept in the front end of the ship way down on the lowermost level, while Dad and I were located a few decks above. Neither location had portholes, and there was no air conditioning. The bunks in our quarters were very close together—stacked in threes—and the place was smelly and stuffy. The only time we used our bunks was at night. The rest of the time we were in other parts of the ship—anyplace but down there. Movies were shown in a large cargo area, and I never missed a chance to see one. Gene Kelly, whom I loved so much in *Anchors Aweigh,* starred in a crime movie called *The Black Hand.* What a surprise it was to see him in such a different role. I still had the image in my head of him wearing a sailor suit and dancing with a cartoon mouse, and it was not easy to accept him in a dramatic part.

Our first stop was Manila, in the Philippine Islands. The trip from Hong Kong took about two days. As we got closer to Manila, the water became bluer and bluer until it was an incredible deep purple color. "Why is the water this color, Daddy?" I asked.

"I suppose that's because it's so deep, Gigi. The water here's about thirty-five thousand feet." Wow! I figured that was almost seven miles of water. I saw flying fishes for the first time and was fascinated as

I watched them skimming over the water's surface, trying to avoid the ship's wake.

To our great disappointment, we were not allowed off the ship at Manila. My parents hadn't thought to get visas, and so we had to remain on board. The weather was impossibly humid and hot—over a hundred degrees outside and much hotter in our sleeping quarters. A couple of my mother's cousins came to the ship, hoping we'd be able to spend the day touring Manila with them. But all we could do was yell back and forth until our voices gave out and their necks developed cramps. To top it all, Bobby broke out in boils—horrible, large, pus-filled pimples all over his body. He was in agony. The ship's doctor gave him some ointment, but the heat and pain were very hard on him.

I spent most of the time on deck in any shady spot I could find. When evening came and we finally set sail, everyone on board was relieved. The moving ship created a wonderful breeze that bathed me with a delicious coolness.

———— * ————

"Mummy, Mummy, look what Daddy's got me!" The words came tumbling out of my mouth as I ran excitedly to my mother. It was the night of my eleventh birthday, and I couldn't wait to show her my present. We were about halfway between Manila and Yokohama, Japan, our next stop. My father had just handed me a paper cup of Neapolitan ice cream and a flat wooden spoon and said, "Happy birthday, Gigi." Such thoughtfulness from my father was totally unexpected, and I was thrilled. He knew how much I loved ice cream, and somehow he had arranged this special surprise for me. It more than made up for the awful food on board. We each had a cup of ice cream on deck that night. "Mummy and Daddy," I said, eating the last delicious spoonful, "this is my best birthday ever."

———— * ————

After docking at Yokohama, we got off the ship and boarded a tour bus for a day of sightseeing in Tokyo. I was excited. This was the first time I had set foot on foreign soil. It was strange at first to walk on land again after spending so many days on a ship. I learned what the expression "sea legs" meant. On our way into Tokyo, I saw some destroyed buildings—evidence of World War II, which had ended less than five years earlier. Traveling all this distance to Japan helped me to understand how widespread the war had been.

We went to the Ginza, the famous shopping area in Tokyo, and then to an art museum. "Is this our new home?" Bobby asked again in a pitiful voice. By now the boils had dried up and he was feeling fine, but he still yearned for a place to call home. Tokyo made no impression on me. It was filled with people, just like Shanghai was, and the shops in the Ginza couldn't match those on Bubbling Well Road or Avenue Joffre.

My parents decided to have lunch at a restaurant in one of the large department stores. While we were waiting for our order, my father, who had excused himself to go to the men's room, returned with someone I had never expected to see again. It was George, my American Army major friend. I was so happy to see him, but I didn't know how to behave. I wanted to throw my arms around him and tell him how much he meant to me, what he had made me realize about myself, but I couldn't.

George picked me up and said how much I'd grown and how happy he was to see me again, too. "Do you remember our day together, Gigi?" he asked, sitting down and putting me on his lap. Did I remember!

"I sure do," I said, feeling awkward. Why had it been so easy to talk with him then? Why was I having such difficulty now? George ate lunch with us, and then it was time to take the bus back to the ship. None of us were ready to go back on board, but we still had the entire Pacific Ocean to cross. I said good-bye to George for the second time, but it was different from before: I didn't cry.

———— * ————

Our journey from Yokohama to Honolulu was rough and stormy the first couple of days. Practically everyone on board became seasick, and I lost all appetite for food.

One day our sleeping quarters started to smell strange. It got so bad that my father and I couldn't stand to be down below anymore, so we moved our bedding and slept up on deck instead. Then one morning we found out the reason. A man had died in a bunk a few feet away from ours. He had been dead for about three days, and what we smelled was his rotting corpse. A funeral was held, and the poor man's body was wrapped in a cloth and buried at sea. The cleaning crew took all his bedding and burned it and used a strong disinfectant to scrub our bathroom.

The first night we went back downstairs to sleep, my father staggered back from the bathroom wheezing and coughing. He was clutching his chest and could barely breathe. Boris and I rushed him to the doctor's office where he was immediately given a shot of adrenalin. Within a few minutes, his breathing became almost normal, but the asthma attack had upset and scared him very much. Something in the disinfectant had triggered the reaction, so, for the next few days, my father had to use a different bathroom.

On May 16 we celebrated Boris's birthday. My father used the twenty dollar bill he had hidden in his lighter to buy some "liquid refreshment," as he put it. Because we crossed the International Date Line the next day, it was May 16 again, so Boris had two birthdays in one year. Of course, Boris, Luba, and my parents had to celebrate it properly once more, so they bought more of the same "refreshment." I envied Boris. Why couldn't we have crossed the International Date Line on my birthday?

———— * ————

Early in the morning of May 18 we docked in Honolulu. Joe Kurlansky, an old Russian friend of my father's, met us at the ship with his fiancée, Helen. Joe and Helen were going to be married the next day. They took us for a lovely day of sightseeing all over the island of Oahu. I could not believe how beautiful everything was, with so many different trees and flowers in bloom. The beaches were wide and sandy, and the water was a beautiful emerald green and very clear. Even though it was sunny, it showered for a few minutes every hour or so. I had never experienced such strange weather, but Joe told us it was typical Hawaiian weather for this time of year.

We went to Waikiki Beach, Diamond Head, the zoo, and the aquarium. We didn't get to see Pearl Harbor, but I was impressed by the size of World War II in the Pacific. I was thousands of miles from Shanghai, yet bombs had fallen here as well.

As our ship pulled away from the dock at sunset, we waved good-bye to Joe and Helen and listened to some musicians playing and singing the song "Aloha Oe"—a farewell song that ended with the words "until we meet again." It was a beautiful way to leave a gorgeous place.

——————— * ———————

On the morning of May 23, 1950, the ship's captain announced we'd be arriving in San Francisco that afternoon. My parents and Boris and Luba had packed up all of our belongings, and we spent most of the time out on deck. The weather was breezy and sunny.

"Watch out for the Golden Gate Bridge, Gigi," my mother said. I had heard all about the famous bridge. It was painted red and had two tall towers. I kept my eyes glued on the horizon and wanted to be sure to spot the bridge as soon as I could. Just as we were passing the rocky Farallon Islands, someone shouted, "There it is!" Was that the Golden Gate Bridge? That large speck way off in the distance? As I was looking ahead, concentrating on the bridge, I heard my mother shout, "Look, Gigi, whales!" I turned and saw her pointing to some large shapes off the ship's side. They were gray whales and looked enormous, yet graceful, as they moved through the water. "Whales are supposed to be good luck," my mother added, hugging me.

We were getting closer to the bridge now, and it got bigger and bigger. How incredible the giant red structure looked, welcoming us to our new home. An American lady said to me, "Young man, would you mind helping me with something?" I didn't know what she wanted, but she started to unfold what looked like a bed sheet. She gave me one end of it to hold and then said, "I told some friends I'd say hello to them from the ship, and this sheet will be my signal to them."

We stretched the plain piece of cloth between us and held it at an angle so that people standing on the bridge could see it. The wind suddenly blew hard, and we had to hang on very tightly. The passengers began cheering as we got closer and closer to the bridge. The level of excitement was so strong I could feel it.

As we sailed under the Golden Gate Bridge into San Francisco Bay, the American lady cried tears of joy, happy to be home again. I began to cry, too, not knowing why. What my parents had longed for and what I had grown to want was actually happening. I was entering a new and unknown world, both scary and exciting at the same time.

The beautiful, hilly, white city of San Francisco was getting closer, and soon we'd be getting off the ship. How different from Shanghai, I thought. What would school be like here? Would the American kids laugh at my British accent? And where would we live? I wondered. A new life lay just ahead of me, and I couldn't wait for it to begin.